Sea Kayaking

Nigel Robinson and Alun Richardson

THE CROWOOD PRESS

First published in 2007 by
The Crowood Press Ltd
Ramsbury, Marlborough
Wiltshire SN8 2HR

British Library Cataloguing-in-Publication Data
A catalogue record for this book is available from the British Library.

ISBN 978 1 86126 827 3

Typeset by Jean Cussons Typesetting, Diss, Norfolk

Printed and bound in Spain by Graphy Cems

CONTENTS

ACKNOWLEDGEMENTS

Many people nowadays are vastly impressed with the greatness of our age, with all the inventions and the progress of which we hear daily, and which appear indisputably to exalt the highly-gifted white race far over all others. These people would learn much by paying close attention to the development of the Eskimos, and to the tools and inventions by aid of which they obtain the necessaries of life among natural surroundings that place such pitifully small means at their disposal.

Fridtjof Nansen from Eskimo Life *(1894)*

We would like to thank the following people for their help with the book: Howard Jeffs for putting his vast knowledge of kayak design to good use in writing the first chapter; Trevor Massiah and Nick Hurst for helping with the photography; Ortlieb for providing a vast array of their excellent dry bags; Nige Dennis Kayaks for providing his superb kayaks; Lendal paddles for supplying paddles; Lesley Jones for her editorial skills; our partners Lesley and Fran plus our children for putting up with the long hours spent putting the book together.

INTRODUCTION

Sea kayaking is probably one of the oldest forms of transport and an environmentally friendly one at that. The Inuit found it crucial to their existence and essential for gathering food. I am sure that at times they marvelled in their ability to travel over the sea under their own steam and to enjoy the incredible emotions that the sea conveys.

In this ever-shrinking world, the sea is one of the last great wilderness areas, and to experience it with the self-sufficiency that sea kayaking offers is a special kind of freedom. Equally, the diversity sea kayaking allows for a great range of opportunities, from long, solo circumnavigations and ground-breaking isolated expeditions, to playing in the rocks and surf or journeying to a remote beach with the family, or simply using the kayak as a platform to observe the fauna and flora offered by the coastal environs.

As sea paddlers we have the ability to travel slowly, quietly and with no trace of our passage, in some of the most beautiful, yet fragile, landscapes in the world; this privilege bears a heavy responsibility. The increased pressure on our coastline has led to an equal pressure to reduce the burden. We have a duty to provide sustainable use of this environment, to abide by management agreements laid down and to participate in the ongoing discussions of minimizing impact on the locations we use and of the concept of 'paddling lightly'. Paddlers are organized into readily defined groups and areas, and are therefore easy targets for those with power to yield. If we do not act in a manner that preserves our coastline for future generations, some less understanding body will do it for us!

The same goes for safety. In the past the Inuit travelled through their inhospitable environment and bore the consequences of their decisions. Today there always seems someone to blame and fatalities in kayaking have a consequence for the rest of the sea-kayaking community. Whilst not wishing to increase the 'nanny state' and to still allow freedom, we still have a duty to abide by certain safety requirements emphasized in this book.

Good paddling!

Nigel and Alun

CHAPTER 1

MINIMUM-IMPACT SEA KAYAKING

'LEAVE NO TRACE'

The impact that sea kayakers have on the sea has to be seen in context. The disturbance we cause is minimal compared to industry and agriculture, but we should not be complacent. Here is some advice to help minimize our impact:

- Plan your route to avoid sensitive natural areas, especially wildlife breeding sites, and bear in mind that these sites may vary with the seasons.
- Learn about the wildlife.
- Pack smart. Take suitable equipment to reduce your reliance on the natural environment – carry a fuel stove, a trowel to bury human waste, a suitable tent and sufficient food and clothing for the season. Discard excess food packaging, that may be left behind as rubbish, before you leave.
- Secure necessary permission to visit restricted areas such as nature reserves or private land.

COMING ASHORE

Much of your unintentional impact occurs when ashore, whether camping overnight or day-tripping, especially in wilderness areas.

- Choose landing and camping sites carefully when planning your route. Plan to use campsites that can accommodate your party size. A maximum of twelve, even less for extended trips, is recommended.

A group of sea kayakers in Romsey Sound.

- Be aware of puffin burrows and avoid getting too close or walking over them.
- Never land on a beach with a colony of breeding seals, except in an emergency.
- On sand dunes and machair, always look and listen for birds, and carry kayaks rather than dragging them.
- Take home all your rubbish, including empty packaging, food scraps and sanitary products. Collect rubbish left by others, if possible. Do not burn cans or plastic.
- Use existing campsites and tracks whenever possible. If visiting a previously undisturbed site, reduce your movement around the area to a minimum. Carry, rather than drag, your kayak.
- Use a fuel stove for cooking.
- Campfires can leave ugly scars, reduce the availability of dead timber as habitat and can escape to start destructive wildfires, so be very careful how and when you light them.
- Be sensitive where you deposit human waste. Burying your waste is a minimum: also consider disposal in the sea or even carrying it out of areas where appropriate disposal is difficult.
- Avoid using soaps or detergent when camping. Beach sand is an excellent alternative for cleaning cookware.

INTERACTING WITH WILDLIFE

Sea kayaks are perfect platforms from which to view our coastal wildlife. Here are some guidelines that will help you to reduce your impact, while still enjoying the wildlife close up:

- A good way to minimize our impact on the sea is to learn more about it. For instance, a knowledge of the breeding seasons of birds and seals will help us to avoid getting too close when they are most sensitive to our presence. A greater understanding will help you to appreciate their behaviour so that you can modify your own to minimize impact.
- Maintain a respectful distance from all wildlife, both on land and water. A rough guide is 50m (165ft) from birds, seals, whales and dolphins, but this will vary with species and the season.
- Do not disturb breeding wildlife. Avoid landing on smaller off-shore islands used for breeding, and camp well away from other breeding sites.

A grey seal. Half of the world's population of grey seals are found on and around British coasts, and numbers here have doubled since 1960.

The common dolphin, found all over the world, travelling in groups of ten to five hundred!

SEA CLIFFS

Cliff-nesting seabirds, such as guillemots, razor-bills and kittiwakes, are most vulnerable when the adults are with their eggs and young chicks. If they are suddenly scared off the ledges they may lose their young, which may fall or be taken by predators. The vulnerable time is mid-May to early July. Move quietly and steadily so as not to panic the birds. Puffins nest in burrows along the tops of cliffs. Walking over a burrow can crush the nest or cause the adult to desert its young, so try to be aware of their presence.

Shingle Shores

Terns, ringed plovers and oyster-catchers all nest on shingle beaches. Care should be taken not to disturb nesting birds on these sites between early May and early July. The eggs and chicks are very well camouflaged against the shingle and are easily trodden underfoot.

Sand Dunes

Take care during stops not to damage vegetation, which is important for stabilizing dunes and for helping them grow. Avoid open fires, which damage the dry vegetation. The western shores of the Hebrides have a unique dune grassland known as machair, which is home to wading birds such as lapwing, ringed plover and dunlin.

Estuaries

The UK's estuaries play host to waders and waterfowl between October and March. Undisturbed feeding and resting may be vital to their survival during the depth of winter. Avoid mudflats and sandbanks with large concentrations of birds.

Seal Colonies

There are two species of seal in UK: the common seal and the grey seal. The common has a small concave nose (like a labrador) and pups from May to July. The grey has a large 'Roman' nose and pups from late August to November, and is the larger and more common species. Avoid beaches with small pups on them, as a sudden disturbance can lead to pups being squashed in the panic or being separated from their parents who may be unable to find them afterwards. Grey seals remain on the beach with their pups for about three weeks, whereas common seals go into the sea almost immediately.

Open Sea

In summer, you may encounter large rafts of duck chicks, mainly of eider or shelduck, accompanied by adult birds. Try to avoid splitting up these rafts as the chicks are vulnerable to predators if they become separated. In late summer they moult and are at their weakest and most vulnerable.

In conclusion, leave everywhere that you travel through in a better condition than when you found it, and develop an empathy for wildlife – after all, if it was not there the coast would be a less interesting place for all of us.

CHAPTER 2

KAYAK DESIGN AND CONSTRUCTION
Howard Jeffs

INTRODUCTION

The modern sea kayak is a far cry from the craft of our predecessors, the Inuit or Eskimo, who evolved and used the kayak (or hunter's boat as it translates) hundreds if not thousands of years ago. Or is it? The Inuit designed a kayak for a specific purpose, possibly to transport their family to a summer camp, but mainly to hunt and survive. The modern sea kayaker also uses the kayak as a tool – thankfully not to pursue wildlife but hopefully to observe it and as a means to travel, whether it be a local day-trip along a short, safe section of coastline or an extended expedition to a remote part of the globe. Just like the Inuit, we have evolved and designed this craft to suit our specific needs.

The range of Inuit kayaks was as vast and as varied as the area of the Northern hemisphere in which they roamed: from the short, stubby kayaks used on rivers and estuaries of North America and Canada to catch caribou (maybe these were the forerunners to our state-of-the-art white water kayaks) to the long, fast, double and three-hole bidarkas used by the Aleutians to travel great distances in search of otters or whale. The latter are now used extensively by tour groups and expeditions because of their vast gear-carrying capacity.

DESIGN

The Inuit

The Inuit designed and built each kayak for the individual who was to use it. Various body measurements would be used to scale up or down specific parts of the craft, bearing in mind its intended purpose. Each group or master kayak builder would have their own design parameters, securely locked in their head, to be passed on to the next generation of builders, usually a son.

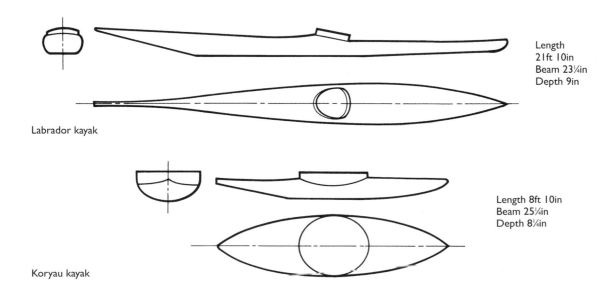

Length
21ft 10in
Beam 23¼in
Depth 9in

Labrador kayak

Length 8ft 10in
Beam 25¼in
Depth 8¼in

Koryau kayak

A 3D line drawing of early sea kayaks.

Modern Times

The range of sea kayaks that are available today is huge – so what should someone new to the sport look for? Designers and manufacturers love to blind us with science – prismatic coefficient this and secondary stability that. All very confusing when one of the virtues of kayaking is its simplicity!

The first question a designer will ask, and anyone considering purchasing a kayak should ask, is: 'What do I want the kayak for?' or 'What do I want to do in this kayak?' Many people have purchased, and will continue to purchase, a kayak because either 'It looks nice' or 'My friend has one, they said it is fantastic!', only to find out later that it is not really suitable to their style or type of paddling.

The only way to find out if a kayak is 'right for you' is to get out and paddle in as many different kayaks as possible – not just in a sheltered bay at a come-and-try-it session held at one of the many sea-kayak symposiums, but at least for a day or possibly longer and in the type of conditions in which you would usually expect to paddle.

Where Does the Design Process Start?

There is no such thing as the perfect kayak, no matter what the designer (who is quite possibly also the salesman) says! The Inuit were halfway there – each kayak unique and built for a particular individual. But with modern manufacturing techniques, the high cost of labour, the limitations of certain materials and the ability to replicate a 'master kayak (pattern)' continuously, everything from here is often a compromise, including the design.

Many designers therefore use computer-aided design packages to assist them, which also speeds up the process, reduces the difficulty in fairing (smoothing out) the line of a hull shape and produces with enviable ease the tedious mathematical calculations that are needed! This said, unless the designer has a feel for the craft and the way it will handle in the conditions or environment for which it is intended, the design will probably be wasted. After all, a seaworthy kayak is what all designers strive to achieve ... is it not?

Design Criteria

With a blank drawing board in front of me I must start with my original questions: 'What is the kayak to be used for?' and 'Who may be using it?'

Rather than delve into the technical and sometimes baffling elements of kayak design, let us take a look at two different designs, consider the various features a designer may encompass

A selection of sea kayaks.

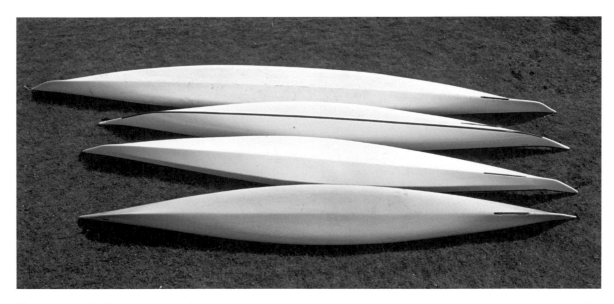

The bottom hull shapes of sea kayaks.

when blending these all together and review the subtle differences that will make the kayaks behave so differently from one another.

THE EXPEDITION KAYAK

This is a single seat, full expedition-style craft, seaworthy, capable of carrying a large amount of equipment, with good directional stability (maintain a straight course) and a fair turn of speed.

THE DAY/WEEKEND KAYAK

This is a single seat, day/weekend touring craft, stable, manoeuvrable and fun to play in the surf, waves or tide races but with enough space to carry overnight gear.

Dimensions

How Long Should the Kayak Be?

It is quite simple: the longer the waterline length of the kayak, the faster it will travel through the water. It is important to remember that it is the waterline length that matters, not just the total hull length. Many kayaks have long, overhanging or sweeping bows and sterns; though these may look elegant and provide other attributes to the design, they can also reduce the potential maximum hull speed. Advertising literature may give the length of a kayak to be 5.5m (18ft), yet its waterline length even when loaded may be

reduced to less that 4.5m (15ft)! Take a look at a marathon or racing kayak, and you will see how the bow and stern are usually vertical in order to maximize the full length of the kayak that is allowed by international rules.

THE EXPEDITION KAYAK

- The main design considerations are: hull speed, directional stability and carrying capacity.
- Usually about 5.5m (18ft) long.
- Volume, and especially its distribution, needs to be carefully considered if the hull speed is to be maintained.

THE DAY/WEEKEND KAYAK

- Manoeuvrability and lively performance is what is required.
- Usually 4.8m (16ft) or less will suffice.
- Subtle shaping of the bow and stern will maintain the waterline length and therefore the speed.

How Wide Should the Kayak Be?

A wide beam does not indicate stability in all conditions! As we shall see later, the cross-sectional shape and, to a degree, the position of the widest point, plays a very important role in directional stability. A marathon-racing kayak is

The cross-sectional shape of a sea kayak.

allowed a minimum beam of 51cm (20in), but this type of craft needs a fair degree of skill to keep upright, especially in the conditions found on open water. As the beam is increased, greater resistance is offered to the forward motion of the craft and this, therefore, starts to have an effect on speed.

THE EXPEDITION KAYAK

- Due to the longer length of the kayak, there is a small gain in lateral (sideways) stability.
- As the kayak is also to be paddled with large amounts of equipment, the centre of gravity will be lowered slightly and this will give the paddler a feeling of stability.
- A beam of about 56cm (22in), depending on the skill of the paddler, is a reasonable compromise here.

THE DAY/WEEKEND KAYAK

- The kayak will usually be paddled empty and therefore it will feel lively and buoyant.

- A beam of around 61cm (24in) will make up for the reduction in length, but any wider may make the kayak feel unstable in rougher conditions.

What Cross-Sectional Shape is Best

The ideal cross-sectional shape for any craft travelling through the water is semicircular, as this gives the least wetted surface area. Sadly, it is also unstable!

If we do the opposite and give the hull a generally rectangular section, though 'initially stable' in calm conditions, it will slowly become unstable as the conditions become more demanding. This is due to the fact that it is a shape that does not fit into the curved surface of a wave and the leverage effect of a wide beam at a low level can encourage capsize. Therefore, a compromise must be found.

The cross-sectional shape changes as it tapers towards the bow and stern; designers will therefore endeavour to keep the shape as fine as possible at the waterline area but increase the volume as it reaches the sides of the deck. This increase in volume will help stop the kayak from plunging in the waves and hopefully will keep the paddler dryer.

THE EXPEDITION KAYAK

- Along with the reduction in beam, a round cross-section will help keep up speed for high, daily mileage.
- Lowering the centre of gravity (seat) may help to compensate for the reduction in stability created by a rounder hull.

THE DAY/WEEKEND KAYAK

- Due to the reduction in length, directional stability (tracking) may be a problem.
- A slight, rounded V cross-section will help this and also give stability in rougher conditions.

Freeboard

Freeboard is the size, shape and area of the kayak above the waterline; it must also be considered when examining a kayak's cross-sectional shape. If the freeboard is increased, it will help to give the kayak more stability as it is heeled over (secondary stability), until the gunwale is submerged and the kayak capsizes. However, the down-side of this is that it will also

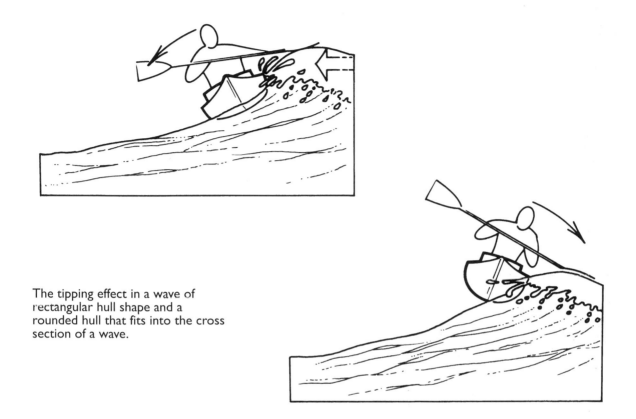

The tipping effect in a wave of rectangular hull shape and a rounded hull that fits into the cross section of a wave.

cause additional 'windage' – the number one enemy of the sea kayaker, affecting the kayak's longitudinal trim and directional stability (*see* Chapter 6). All sea kayaks will suffer from this, but some to a greater degree than others. Therefore the volume above the water and the design of the deck also need the same amount of careful attention that the hull automatically receives!

Many designs are now offered in a high, standard or low freeboard option. Think carefully on the type of paddling you expect to do and make sure that you try the variations out before you commit your cash. Many a fine-looking kayak has turned into a 'beast' once the wind has piped up!

Plan Shape

If we could look up through the water and see the outline of the hull shape, the position of the widest point and the location of the seat, it would give us a considerable amount of information on how the kayak may handle, especially its directional stability.

A symmetrical kayak will have the seat in the centre of the boat and its widest point around the area of the hips. This will give a neutral feel and is found in many general-purpose types of craft. As the widest point is moved towards the stern ('Swedish form'), it will help the design have a fine entry to the water and hopefully maintain boat speed (look at racing kayaks). The aft position of the paddler's weight will also tend to encourage the kayak to keep turning once initiated, especially if the kayak is edged/tilted at the same time.

If the widest point is moved towards the bow ('fish form'), the kayak's centre of gravity and 'pivot point' move forward. This can help the kayak track, however some designers feel that a fish-form shape slows the kayak down.

It must be remembered that plan shape is not everything. By moving the paddler's weight fore or aft, this will affect the trim (the amount the bow is pushed down or lifted up) of the kayak; this must be balanced by distributing the kayak's buoyancy equally fore and aft.

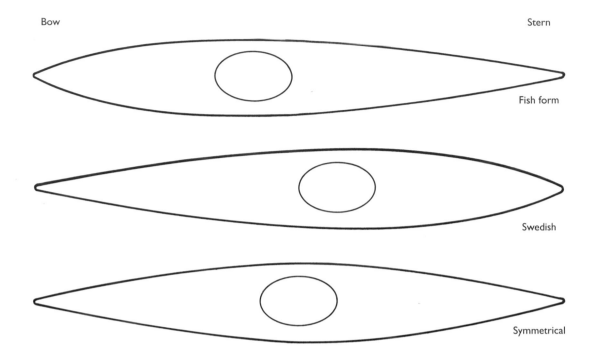

Plan shape.

Rocker Line

Of equal importance to the plan shape is the rocker line. The rocker line is the shape of the bottom of the hull when viewed from the side. If the rocker line is straight (flat), for example on a white-water racing kayak, then the waterline length will be longer, which will not only help towards boat speed but also straighter running (tracking). As the ends of the rocker line are bent upwards, there is a gain in manoeuvrability but a loss in directional stability and speed.

THE EXPEDITION KAYAK

A fast hull form is important and as most turning or course correction will be done by edging/tilting the kayak, 'Swedish form' combined with a straighter rocker line is possibly the best option here. Careful distribution of buoyancy and deck design will help keep the fine bow section dry.

THE DAY/WEEKEND KAYAK

The increase in volume of a 'fish form' kayak's bow section will hopefully help keep the paddler dryer in this shorter boat. Balancing this with a more pronounced rocker line will give a good compromise between speed and manoeuvrability.

Skegs and Rudders

As already mentioned, wind is the number one enemy when kayaking, especially if it is blowing over the rear quarter of the kayak. Depending on the design, the kayak will usually try to turn into the wind, this is known as 'broaching'. Designers will adopt a number of options to try and compensate for this annoying feature, and as always they are all a compromise!

Fixed Skeg

A fixed skeg is part of the original hull design, forming an extension of the keel and a flattening of the rocker at the rear of the kayak. The great advantage to this type of skeg is that there is little that can go wrong with it; however, some care is needed when launching and landing. The disadvantage is that the kayak will run true in most conditions and there will be a marked difference in 'close quarters' manoeuvrability, i.e. an inability to turn tightly.

However, remember that up to a given surface area, a fixcd skeg will only have an optimum effectiveness in a given wind speed/sea state depending on its size. Once this optimium has been exceeded, the broaching effect (turning into the wind) will increase dramatically and, in some cases, the kayak will possibly turn downwind, making matters even worse!

Retractable Skeg
Most kayaks come with a retractable skeg as standard; it does not impede the manoeuvrability of the kayak, while allowing the paddler to compensate for the effect of the wind. The retractable skeg is fitted at the rear of the kayak, but now takes the form of a pivoting blade that can be retracted into the hull (skeg box) or lowered in increments. In doing so, it creates resistance and stops the rear of the kayak sliding around and causing a broach. The great advantage to this system is that it is infinitely adjustable. It is not an up/down, on/off device! Therefore the paddler MUST learn how to 'tune' (adjust) the skeg so that the kayak becomes balanced in the given conditions and direction to the wind. If the paddler then changes course, then the skeg will need to be retuned for the new heading.

The disadvantage to the retractable skeg is its operating system, which will inevitably involve an adjusting wire, rope, elastic or even a

Sea kayak skegs.

Sea kayak rocker lines.

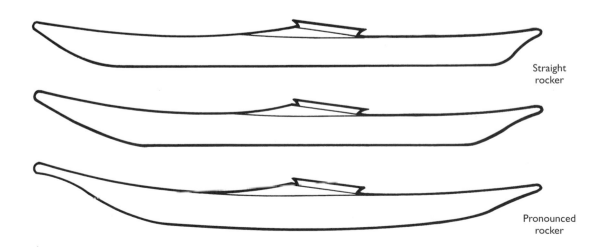

Straight rocker

Pronounced rocker

Skeg controls.

hydraulic system! Obviously these systems can malfunction and cause problems on and off the water. The other disadvantage to the retractable skeg is that it can become jammed with sand, gravel or very small stones. A small piece of strong string threaded through a small hole at the back rear edge of the skeg can help this problem; however, one ingenious designer has now off-set the whole skeg assembly to the side of the hull with no detrimental effects to performance.

Despite these precautions and modifications, it is always advisable to test your skeg for full up and down movement every time you launch on the water.

Rudders

Some sea kayaks come with, or have the facility to 'add on' later, a rudder, which aids manoeuvrability. The great advantage to using a rudder is the increased manoeuvrability, especially during tight turns, or helping to keep the kayak on course. However, just like the retractable skeg, they all have various operating systems to raise and lower the rudder blade; as well as this there are also operating wires connecting the foot operating system to the rudder stock that effects the turning movement, all of which can fail! Therefore it is vital that the paddler can competently handle the kayak in all conditions, with or without the rudder. If opting for a kayak that has a rudder, consider the following two points:

- Has the rudder been fitted to the kayak to make up for a poor design performance?
- Does the foot operating system still allow the paddler to 'brace' their body in the kayak and/or allow the padding energy to be effectively transferred into the forward momentum of the kayak? Many sliding pedal systems do not!

There is no such thing as a perfect kayak! These are personal views and if you speak to another designer, they may paint a very different picture.

CONSTRUCTION

As discussed earlier, the Inuit built their kayaks to fit an individual paddler. The frame was carefully made from the limited timber available and then covered in sealskin. Following the Second World War, kayaks were produced in a similar fashion, but treated canvas was used instead of sealskin. These craft reached their peak in the 1960s with the range of kayaks designed by Percy Blandford, known as PBKs. Around this time, glass reinforced plastic (GRP), more commonly known as fibreglass, appeared on the market and was readily taken up by enthusiastic amateurs as well as professionals who produced all manner of craft.

Following the TV series *Do It Yourself* by Barry Bucknell, the 'Mirror' dinghy was created using plywood with GRP tape to hold the various panels together (known as 'stitch and tape'). This also became popular in the kayaking world,

and variations of the technique are still used today.

GRP involves a range of glass reinforcement and liquid polyester resin being worked by hand into a female mould. The addition of a catalyst causes the resin to set hard and produces a light, strong and ridged shell that is ideal for a kayak. The advantage of GRP is the ability to produce accurate replicas of an original kayak with ease

One of the first commercially available sea kayaks was a replica of a West Greenland kayak brought back by Ken Taylor. Known as the Anas Acuta, it is still manufactured today.

The advent of specialist 'aerospace' materials, such as epoxy resin, Kevlar and carbon fibre, coupled with foam cores and compressed using vacuum pressure, has brought the kayak into the modern age. Very strong, yet light and with increased rigidity, the improvements are dramatic! However, these improvements come at a price, a very expensive price!

In the early 1980s, polyethylene first appeared on the paddling scene. A powdered linear (molecules in a straight line with no cross-linking between the molecules) plastic is poured into an aluminium mould, heated to a high temperature and then tilted end to end whilst being rotated to distribute the liquid plastic. Once cooled it produces a cheap, tough kayak shell that was ideal for white-water kayaks. Unfortunately it is very difficult to structurally bond anything to this material and it was not until the mid 1990s that a commercially viable sea kayak was produced.

Plastic in its many forms is now the most popular material for kayaks. However, for the dedicated paddler, GRP remains the choice due to the ability to personally customize the craft to an individual's needs, even if it is a little more expensive!

CHAPTER 3

GETTING STARTED

Some people start sea kayaking by the 'trial and error method' – they read a book such as this, buy a kayak and some ancillary equipment, and away they go. This method may well suit some people, however, it is well proven that by receiving good coaching and feedback, the process of learning is accelerated and avoids falling into bad habits/practice, which are harder to break later. Participating with peers and coaches will also allow the novice to learn by watching, listening and doing. It can also increase their motivation and enjoyment of the sport during the initial stages.

The British Canoe Union (BCU) runs an accreditation scheme for centres and clubs. The BCU is the national governing body for all paddle sports (sea, river, kayak, canoe, slalom, racing and even sailing) in the UK. Whether a centre is accredited will depend on the qualifications held by the coaches and the kit provided. Other countries will also offer this service, for example the American Canoe Association and Irish Canoe Union. By learning at an accredited centre or club, it also means you can try the sport without being caught in the minefield of purchasing equipment before you really know what you need or where to start, or even whether you like it!

The best way to receive up-to-date and safe coaching is to look for a National Governing Body (NGB) trained and assessed coach. Under BCU schemes, coaches undergo training and assessment to enable them to coach and guide; they are referred to as level 1, 2, 3, 4 or 5 coaches, depending on the training, knowledge and experience they have. The award will not only dictate the experience of coaching they have but also the environment and conditions that they can operate in, for example a level 1 coach is limited to extremely sheltered waters such as a swimming pool or canal, whereas a level 5 sea coach has no limitations where they can go on the sea.

PURCHASING EQUIPMENT

When purchasing equipment take advice from impartial kayakers before visiting a shop. Do not be afraid to buy second-hand, as long as you know the age and usage of a piece of kit. The first items to buy are those that are personal and cannot normally be borrowed, for example thermal clothing and footwear, then work your way to buying kit that makes your paddling more comfortable.

PROTECTIVE EQUIPMENT

Today, paddlers are lucky to benefit from a wide range of equipment supported by extensive research. The sea can be an unforgiving environment and it is important to dress according to the water/air temperature, the wind and weather. Thought must also be given as to how much time may be spent in the water. If in doubt, dress for the worst-case scenario, in other words, cold and wet! Look for garments that have reinforcing patches at high wear areas, the elbows, bum seat and knees. Remember to allow room for extra clothing to be worn underneath.

Wetsuits

These are ideal when the paddler is likely to end up in the sea. As the name implies, wetsuits work by trapping a layer of water, which is subsequently warmed by the body. Unfortunately, when not wet, they can be uncomfortable and irritate the skin. The most common type of wetsuit worn by sea paddlers is the long johns (trouser and bib). Wetsuits also come as full-piece suits, which are very warm when wet but restrict movement more. They come in a variety of thicknesses in the arms and the body, 3–4mm (⅛ in) is the norm. A smooth outer coating to the neoprene will help prevent evaporation exacerbated by the wind. The long johns wetsuit is normally worn with layers of clothing on the upper body, with a wind/waterproof cagoule over the top.

Heading for Bardsey Island off the Lleyn Peninsula; paddler Anna Williams.

A wetsuit long-john keeps the paddler warm when wet.

The Layering System

The concept of the 'layer system' has been around for some time. The idea is that a number of thin clothing layers are warmer and less bulky than one or two thicker items. By wearing layers, the wearer has more scope to adjust their temperature by removing or adding clothing. Generally paddlers start with a thermal vest, then a thin fleece and then, when cold, a thicker fleece.

Materials

The best insulation against the cold and wet is provided by polyester, nylon or wool. Cotton garments can provide cooling/sun protection when it is hot and the water is warm. Fleece technology can be divided into base, mid and outer layers, depending on their thickness. The advantage of synthetic layers is that they are warm, even when wet, and they dry more quickly.

Protecting the Extremities

One-third of our body heat is lost through our heads, therefore, headwear is vital. A balaclava, 'beanie' or neoprene hood works well when it is cold; when the sun is out, a sun hat or rain hat is essential (make sure they do not constantly fall over your eyes).

Handwear is available in two options: neoprene gloves, which are warm but restrict movement, or pogues. The latter are tubes of nylon or neoprene that velcro over the paddle shaft, allowing the hand to grip normally, without restriction. Neoprene pogues hold their shape and can make them easier to put on and take off.

At the very least, the paddler should wear some form of footwear, e.g. old trainers or sandals to prevent cuts to the feet. These can be

The layering system (and pages 24–25).

The layering system *(continued)*.

worn with neoprene socks for warmth or, better still, a pair of neoprene boots, the soles of which should be thick enough to provide comfort on sharp rocks.

Cagoules (Cags)/Outer Shells

These come in a variety of designs and form the outer shell of the layering system. Some have short sleeves, some long, they can be dry or semi-dry and can even come with a spray deck sewn onto the bottom (a cag-deck). Essentially they are designed to keep the wind out, which reduces wind chill and hopefully keeps the water out!

Inexpensive ones are made from polyurethane or neoprene-proofed nylon, and more expensive models from a breathable fabric, such as Gortex. They should have taped seams to stop water entering through the stitching. The neck and wrist seals can either be made from neoprene or latex, the former is easy to fit but only latex or a semi latex, which is harder to get on, will keep the water out. Some manufacturers use both seal types, which will keep the wrists and neck warmer.

For the sea paddler, latex wrist seals will keep the sea out and a second wrist seal will help keep the blood in the forearm warm. The waist should have a twin seal for under and over the spray deck. A hood is very useful as long as there is a second semi-dry neck seal underneath.

The layering system *(concluded)*.   *ABOVE AND RIGHT:* **Other options for layering.**

Waterproof Trousers and Salopettes

These are designed with the same fabrics and seals as cagoules, and come as trousers or a trouser and bib combination (salopettes). The advantage of salopettes is that when the paddler is seated, the small of the back is kept drier and warmer, and the torso has an extra layer of insulation.

Dry Suits

With the advance of modern materials, dry suits have become a realistic and affordable alternative. The advantages are that they keep water out and are less restrictive. A slight disadvantage that a dry suit has is that it is easily damaged and the slightest tear will let water in. A distinct disadvantage is that it is difficult to go to the toilet, but it is possible to have a pee-zip fitted.

Entry zips can be across the shoulders or diagonally across the front of the body. The latter is easier to fasten. Some manufacturers include a twin seal for the spray deck and Gortex or latex socks.

Always remember to vent a dry suit prior to paddling, otherwise an immersion in the sea will result in air tracking up the legs and the paddler floating upside down. To vent, hold open the neck and crouch down, thus squeezing all the air through the neck seal. A breathable fabric, although more expensive, will help to prevent the body becoming warm and sweaty!

Neoprene pogues – the best thing to keep hands warm in a cold wind.

Trousers and salopette combination.

Cagoules/outer shell garments.

A dry suit.

Helmets

Helmets are not always required when paddling in calm or deep water, however, they may become a necessity when landing on a rocky shore or negotiating caves or narrow passages. Helmets come in two broad designs:

- a full helmet that extends over the ears;
- one that just protects the skull only.

Inside, they are either all foam, in which case the wearer has to buy the correct size or foam combined with a cradle, which can be adjusted to fit the head. Generally, the greater the thickness of foam, the greater the shock absorption between the outer shell and the paddler's head.

PERSONAL FLOTATION DEVICES (PFDS)

PFDs can be split into two categories: buoyancy aids and lifejackets.

Buoyancy Aids

A buoyancy aid wraps around the body providing insulation and armour; it also allows a greater degree of mobility than a lifejacket, especially when the paddler finds themselves in the water. Buoyancy aids come in a wide variety of styles, shapes and sizes.

Look for the following aspects in a sea-kayaking buoyancy aid:

- a short torso;
- ample arm cut-away to enable unrestricted paddling;
- at least one pocket, ideally on the front, to stow safety kit, e.g. a flare;
- a zip that enables the buoyancy aid to be put on and off more easily;
- adjustable straps to allow extra clothing to be worn;
- durable construction;
- a CEN number or Kitemark;
- reflective tape strips.

Fitting the Buoyancy Aid
A buoyancy aid is only effective when it is sized and fitted correctly. To test the correct fit, hold your arms straight out and have a friend lift the buoyancy aid by the shoulder straps; if it slips upwards, tighten the straps. It should also not rub around the chin or armpits.

Two types of kayak helmet.

Care and Maintenance
Over time the foam in a buoyancy aid ages and shrinks – check it before purchase.

- Do not permanently alter a buoyancy aid, if it does not fit with all the straps adjusted, then a different one is required.
- It is not a kneeling pad or cushion.
- Wash and dry it before storing in a well-ventilated place away from direct sunlight.
- Never dry one directly on a heat source.
- Check the buoyancy aid regularly for defects and when necessary, for buoyancy, i.e. jump in the water – does it still bring you to the surface?

Lifejackets

Lifejackets are fundamentally designed to keep the wearer upright with their face out of the water. Their construction can be either foam, foam and inflatable pouches or fully inflatable. The first two types tend to be very bulky and reduce mobility; they are generally not worn by paddlers because they hinder swimming or getting back into a kayak. The third type is more compact and is inflated by triggering a gas cylinder, either manually or automatically, on contact with water. They can also be inflated by mouth.

Dry Bags

The advent of welded and taped seams has allowed manufacturers to produce a flexible and light dry bag. When the top is carefully rolled down and the fastex buckle secured, the contents will stay dry. Ortlieb have perfected a range

A lifejacket, buoyancy aid and an inflated lifejacket.

The superb Ortlieb
range of dry bags
and wallets.

Neoprene nylon spray decks.

of bags and wallets that can protect small to large items, from sleeping bags to charts.

Spray Decks, Splash Skirts

These are available in nylon, neoprene and a combination of the two.

Nylon

These are cheap and easy to put on and take off, and will fit a range of sizes of kayak cockpits; however, water can pool on the top and they can be easily ripped off by waves crashing onto the deck. They are suitable for beginners

Neoprene

The fit of neoprene spray decks is very tight, water is less likely to pool on the surface, plus they are warmer and less prone to imploding when a waves crashes on them. More advanced paddlers will prefer neoprene or similar spray decks. The down side to neoprene is that, unless wetted first, they are difficult to put on.

Before buying a neoprene spray check, consider the make of the kayak because the spray deck must accurately match the cockpit and also the chest size of the paddler. Some paddlers find that neoprene is too warm and restricts their movements.

PADDLES

Historically, Inuit (Eskimo) paddles were made from driftwood, the length of which determined the size of the paddles; they also tended to have long thin blades that required a low horizontal paddling style. Today's range of materials and construction techniques provide the paddler with an overwhelming choice according to their paddling needs.

In the past, a very crude method of fitting the paddle to the paddler was to stand the paddle upright, reach up with the hand and grip the top of the blade with a straight arm. Today, choice can be refined by the paddler considering the following: the paddle is made up of two main components: the blade and the shaft. The relationship between the two is very important, depending on the size and age of the paddler and the use that the paddle is put to. For example, surfing, which requires a short burst of power, would use a big blade and short shaft; a young or smaller paddler may use a smaller blade and shorter shaft.

Construction

- Wooden laminate paddles are warm to hold but they can be heavy.
- Plastic blades are durable and cheap but lack rigidity.
- Aluminium shafts are cheap and strong, and they are often covered with a plastic coating that can tear or chip causing blisters. Aluminium also oxidizes and corrodes in seawater.

Composite construction means that the blade and/or the shaft is composed of more than one material. This can be glass fibre, resin, carbon or nylon in the blades. Carbon fibre is light and strong, but when made from 100 per cent carbon fibre they are very rigid. Rigid blades do not flex, resulting in an increased risk of injury to wrists and elbows. By reducing the carbon fibre content, and adding nylon/glass fibre, flexibility is improved and the chance of injury reduced. The durability of the blade is also improved.

A range of Lendal paddles.

Size of Paddles

In much the same way as we use small cogs on a bike to accelerate and large cogs to cruise, the size of a paddle will change how we paddle.

Acceleration   Cruising

$\longleftrightarrow$

Requires	Requires
Big blades/short shaft	Small blades/long shaft

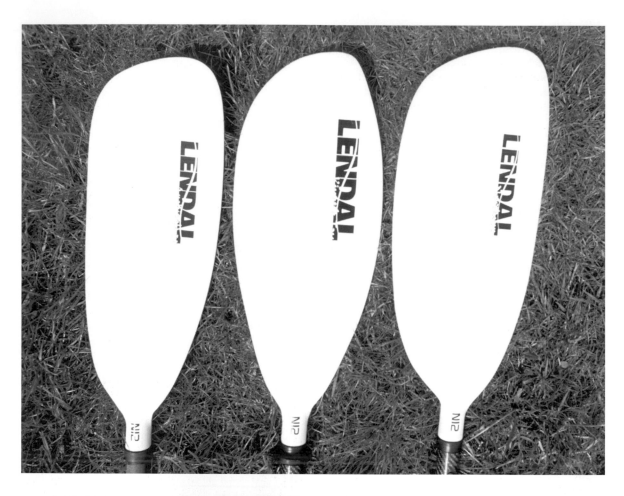

ABOVE: Paddle blades. The size of a blade is defined by its surface area.

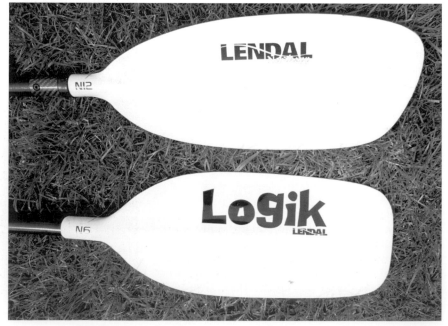

RIGHT: Symmetric (bottom) and asymmetric paddle blades.

The Blade

The blade comes in a variety of shapes and sizes.

Size: the key is the surface area of the blade. A greater surface area will require greater effort to pull it through the water.

Shape: there are two broad shapes:

- Symmetric – both sides of the blade are the same. This can result in 'fluttering', which can lead to repetitive stress injury.
- Asymmetric – one edge is longer than the other. This means that when the blade is placed in the water, the force is equal on the upper and lower edges, stabilizing the blade and reducing 'fluttering'.

Feather: this is the angle that one blade is set in relation to the other: zero feather blades are parallel whereas 90-degree blades are set at right angles to each other. A 90-degree feather was originally designed to reduce resistance to the wind of the dry blade (the blade out of the water) when paddling into a strong headwind. The wrist of the control hand is responsible for twisting the shaft to present each blade to the water. A downside of a 90-degree feather is that the wrist has to be bent acutely and this can cause repetitive strain injury. When wind resistance is not an issue, such as when paddling downwind, the paddler can reduce the feather to reduce wear and tear on their wrist. The degree of feather needed is also governed by the amount of shaft rotation gained from the bending of the elbow.

Left and right feather: most paddlers have a natural bias to their predominant control hand (the hand that twists the shaft). To find out whether the paddle is left-handed, place the power or drive face of the blade against your toes with the shaft upright, whichever direction the other blade drive face faces, determines whether it is right or left.

The Shaft

Grip

This is the bump or flattening in the shaft that is tailored to the palm of the hand. It informs the paddler that their hand is in the correct position (usually the knuckle and the top edge of the blade are in line). There is usually only one grip on the control-hand side of the shaft. The grip can be especially important when finding the correct orientation of the paddle for rolling.

Tenosynovitis

This is the inflammation of tendon sheaths at the wrist, which can be very painful and difficult to cure. Prevention is the best cure – reduce excessive wrist movement by checking technique, reducing blade feather and using a modified crank shaft.

Modified Crank

A paddle shaft with a modified crank puts the blade and shaft in a stable position when the blade enters the water; this reduces the sideways bending of the wrist, therefore alleviating strain and providing a more relaxed grip. Because of the stability of the blade due to the 'castor' action (*see* diagram overleaf), the angle of attack is less critical. This gives increased confidence in rough water and reduces fatigue. It is important when purchasing the modified crank that the paddler's thumb-to-thumb width (taken from holding a straight shaft) is obtained.

Lendal Paddlok system.

Split Paddles and Variable Joint

For ease of carrying as spares or on aeroplanes, paddle shafts can be split in two or even three pieces. The Lendal 'Paddlok' system even has detachable blades. Normally the two halves are inserted in one of three positions: flat, left- or right-handed. Lendal has also developed the variable joint, which allows the paddler to alter the feather of the blades and the length of shaft. This excellent feature allows the paddler to alter the paddles according to the conditions they are paddling in or, as a coach, to enable students to try a range of sizes; add to this interchangeable blades, and you have the ultimate variable paddle.

Choosing a Paddle

A novice should look for a nylon asymmetric blade on a glass fibre/composite shaft, approximately 210cm (83in) long with a 65-degree feather, as a relatively inexpensive option.

SAFETY EQUIPMENT

A common message throughout this book is that having the correct safety equipment does not result in automatic safety. A GPS, EPIRB, VHF radio or mobile phone does not guarantee a rescue. They are simply aids, not the first line of defence. Prevention is better than cure! No rules or technology can replace the need to be watchful for changes in the sea state and the wind direction/strength. While there are always factors beyond our control, like the weather changing, we can cut down on the risks dramatically by common-sense actions, such as checking the weather forecast and tide tables, being aware of local hazards, wearing a PFD, having the required safety gear, taking some lessons and paddling with a partner. Many of these topics are covered in other chapters, here we look at the equipment that will aid the paddler to be self-reliant and minimize the need for external rescue and to allow you to cope in a crisis.

Lendal cranked shafts and the 'crank principle'. Imagine the circle is a freewheeling castor. (Courtesy of Lendal Products Ltd. and Alistair Wilson.)

Advice for Safety Equipment

- Is it waterproof? Ensure that safety kit is kept dry.
- Is it well maintained? Have you checked it recently?
- Is it accessible? Always ensure that you know where the kit is. The paddler should be able to access the kit solo and minimize the risk of compromising the watertight integrity of the kayak, i.e. taking off the spray deck or opening the large hatches.
- Will it get washed/blown away? Kit should either be contained or tied to the person or kayak.
- Is the kit multi-functional, i.e. can it be used for anything else?

Lendal Variable
joint.

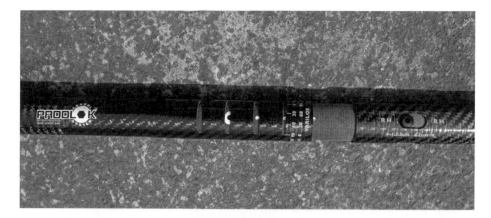

Deck bag/safety
kit.

Equipment failure is often the result of old age, poor maintenance or misuse; therefore ensure that the majority of your equipment is of high quality and well maintained. When looking at safety equipment, it is beneficial to look at what incidents we might have to deal with, rather than carry large amounts of kit just in case! These lists are not exhaustive and they may vary depending on the area of the world in which you paddle.

Equipment for all the following incidents is kept either on deck, in a deck bag or in the PFD.

- Broken or lost paddle: carry split paddles as a spare set.

- Leaking kayak: carry plumber's tape (webbing impregnated with putty) and epoxy putty; both of these work on damp surfaces. Gaffer/duck tape will also repair small leaks if the surface is dried before application. Some sea kayakers have integral foot or hand pumps that can be operated with the spray deck in place. Gaining in popularity is the use of portable hand pumps with the advantage that they can be used in unfamiliar kayaks and can be passed to other kayakers to pump out their kayak.

- Problems with skegs or footrests: carry a multi-tool that includes knife and pliers, spare footrest bolts, string and elastic.

A portable pump in use with the advantage that it can be passed from kayak to kayak.

- Lost or leaking hatch cover: carry a spare or a piece of polythene that can be kept in place by a length of elastic.
- Blisters, cuts and grazes: carry electrical insulation tape – any other tape or plaster will come off the skin too easily when wet.
- Sunburn: carry a small tube of high-factor sun cream and some lip protection.

For the following problems, carry kit in the day hatch just behind the cockpit:

- Damaged spray deck: carry a spare nylon deck that will easily fit over the existing deck. Also carry a strong needle and thread and gaffer tape.

- Extensive damage to the kayak: dependent on the length or remoteness of the trip, fibreglass resin, hardener and cloth can be carried. Care should be taken to isolate these ingredients from each other and other kit – small screw-topped plastic bottles with taped lids seems to work best. Always use surgical type gloves when applying it. In addition, carry assorted cable ties, sandpaper, wire and glue.
- Hypothermia: carry kit that will allow the paddler to continue until shelter is reached, when more clothing can be gained from the main hatches. Carry spare clothes, especially a hat and paddling mitts, bivvy bag open at both ends or a large cagoule.

- Tiredness: carry spare food and water, and a towline.
- Injury: carry a simple first-aid kit (*see* Chapter 7).

EQUIPMENT FOR ATTRACTING ATTENTION

Flares

There are two types of flares: handheld and aerial.

Handheld

- Orange hand-smoke: these are for day use only; visibility 4km (2.5 miles), duration 60s.
- Red hand-flare: these are for day or night use; visibility 10km (6 miles) at night, duration 60s.

Both are useful for attracting attention and guiding a rescue craft or helicopter to your position.

Aerial Flares

- Para red distress rocket: day or night use; visibility 15km (9 miles) day, 40km (25 miles) night, duration 40s.

Understand how to use them before they are required; it would make the situation more stressful if you were trying to decipher the instructions in a rough sea.

- Never fire an aerial flare if a helicopter is arriving.
- If there is no wind, fire the flare vertically; if it is windy, fire downwind at an angle of 15 degrees; and if the cloud is low, fire at 45 degrees.
- Always ensure that flares that can be seen during the day and the night are carried. It is a good idea to carry a double-ended flare, a red pinpoint and smoke, on your PFD or bum bag in case you are parted from the kayak. Also carry one of each type in the kayak. Remember they are only useful if they work, so ensure they are in date.

Whistle

A whistle should be attached to the buoyancy aid. Whistles can be useful to attract the attention of another kayaker.

Light/Strobe

A high-visibility, waterproof, flashing light will make it easier for a rescue crew to pinpoint someone at night.

Snap Light or Cylume

These are tubes that contain two chemicals. When mixed, usually by bending, they glow in a variety of colours for up to 12h. They are very useful for identifying group members at night whilst preventing loss of night vision. They can be strapped to a helmet to make it simple to count heads.

Light sticks.

An *Aide-Mémoire*

- Map/chart.
- Tide table.
- Compass.
- Shelter.
- First-aid kit.
- Repair kit.
- Hot drink.
- Whistle.
- Towline.
- Pump.
- Spare food.
- Flares.
- Spare paddles.
- Lunch.
- Torch.
- Spare clothes.
- Money.
- Dry bags.

- PFD.
- Cagoule.
- Wet suit or dry suit.
- Spray deck.
- Helmet.
- Knife.
- Gloves and hat.
- Sun hat.
- Sunscreen.
- Lip salve.
- Water.
- Throw line.
- VHF radio.
- Flares.
- Binoculars.
- Sunglasses.
- Camera.

Marine VHF Radio

Anyone who does a significant amount of sea paddling should consider carrying a marine VHF radio (mobile phones have limited reception at sea). For obvious reasons, sea paddlers are limited to using handheld radios with integral battery packs. Most handheld radios have a radio frequency output of 4–6W and have a power-saving function for short-range communications rated at 1W, i.e. they use less power.

Radio waves bend with the curve of the earth slightly and can bounce off some surfaces, such as mountains, but VHF is more or less 'line of sight', so the higher the antenna, the greater the range. When talking to someone in another kayak, the effective range is approximately 8–13km (5–8 miles). Coastguards generally put their more powerful and sensitive transceiver antenna on top of the highest point possible to increase the range to 32–48km (20–30 miles).

Paddlers can increase their antenna height, if possible, by climbing a hill, which can make a significant difference, but is not always practical, especially if the radio is needed while on the water. A large swell can also make reception intermittent.

A major problem with any electrical equipment is exposure to salt and moisture. Most good-quality radios are water 'resistant' and some even waterproof. However, despite these claims use a 'waterproof' bag. There are some that are designed to keep the radio dry, accessible and allow operation without taking the unit out of the bag.

VHF radios have other functions, such as memory, scan and tri-watch, but the only one you definitely need is an instant push-button access to channel 16, as well as a full complement of all marine channels, including weather.

Battery Life
Few places at sea have facilities to recharge batteries, so carry extra battery packs, either another rechargeable or a battery pack that takes standard AA batteries. On a power per size basis, there is generally more power with standard alkaline AA batteries, and it is easy to carry lots of extras. Not all models of radios have alkaline battery-pack options. Always keep a fully charged battery attached for use in case of an emergency.

Using the receiver does not use much power so a battery may last for weeks just listening to daily weather reports. Transmitting, however, uses lots of power. Depending on the battery it could be flat in 20–30min unless the low-power saving function is used.

Licence/Training
The simple answer is that anyone using a VHF radio requires a licence. However, the paddler is unlikely to get into trouble if simply using it to call in an emergency and listen to weather broadcasts. The advantage of a licence is that the radio can then be used to communicate more

easily and the training received is very useful; plus the licence is for life.

Operating a VHF

Read the instructions, but here are some tips:

- Before you transmit, make sure the frequency you are using is not being used or use channel 16 for the coastguard.
- Hold the microphone a few inches away from your mouth and speak slowly and clearly, repeating the destination and your identification three times, because the receiving station might not be receiving a strong signal, e.g. 'Milford Haven coastguard, Milford Haven coastguard, Milford Haven coastguard this is X kayak group, X kayak group, X kayak group'.
- Do not shout! Screaming will distort the transmission, making it unintelligible

Channels

Avoid talking unnecessarily between kayaks and never use channel 16 – the most important channel for all mariners because it is the international distress and calling frequency. Channel 16 is also used to supply mariners with up-to-date weather forecasts, which is very useful at sea. In an emergency use channel 16 to establish initial contact with anyone who answers. It is likely that the coastguard will hear the call and will direct you to another channel; if they do not, then hopefully other boats in the area will have heard you and answer (switch them to another channel for conversation), but remember to go back to channel 16 in case the coastguard is hailing you. Flares should be used to help them locate you but remember they only last for 60s. It is important that you communicate effectively, it might be difficult for someone sitting miles away at a coastguard station or on a cruise ship to appreciate the conditions and seriousness of the situation.

Using Channel 16

If you are in a life-threatening situation, the phrase to say is 'Mayday, Mayday, Mayday' and state the following:

- how many craft, type of craft and how many people are in the group;
- position (as accurate as possible);
- the problem, e.g. heart attack, one man in the water;

- intended course of action.

Give further information whenever asked, but do not let talking on the radio interfere with immediate safety needs. Any rescuer will assume that you are unable to talk and will continue with the rescue process, as long as they have an idea what is happening and where. When your hands are free again, get back on the radio with more information, if needed. A Mayday call is serious because all available resources will be alerted, whether it is calling out a helicopter or diverting a nearby cruise ship to the position given. However, do not delay a rescue call even if there is uncertainty of it being needed, valuable time could be wasted. If it turns out that outside help is not needed, the rescue can always be called off.

EPIRB

EPIRB is the acronym for 'emergency position indication radio beacons', and these are a good idea on a trip in an isolated area or if paddling well out to sea.

Older 121.5/243MHz EPIRBs

Those manufactured or sold prior to February 1990 were designed to be detected by over-flying search aircraft, not by satellite detection. Therefore the stability and accuracy of the transmissions were not critical factors. Nowadays, not all aircraft monitor the 121.5/243 MHz frequencies, thus detection is either via chance or by a search aircraft on a full-scale search. After February 1990, EPIRBS are detected by satellite. However, two satellite passes are required to fix a position and then this is only accurate to within 20km (12.5 miles). If you have one of these older units you are not as likely to be rescued.

Modern 406MHz EPIRBs

The COSPOS/SARSAT system was designed for EPIRBs operating on 406MHz using digital signals. All 406MHz EPIRBs sold are compatible with this SARSAT system. They can be detected to an accuracy of within 5km (3 miles) and can also identify the EPIRB through an international registration system. Thus they would know they are looking for a kayak instead of a container ship. Some EPIRBs also have the capability of indicating the type of distress, such as medical, collision and so on.

CHAPTER 4

GOING TO SEA

The Six Ps – Prior Planning and Preparation Prevents Poor Performance

There are many paddlers who have ventured out to sea with little or no planning at all, and returned safely, but their success probably has more to do with luck than expertise on their part. It may appear to the uninitiated that experienced paddlers do little planning when in fact it is all being done in their head, a process that takes many years of experience.

Planning is essential, even if it just confirms what is already known, such as the tide will push us along, but it may also prevent a trip becoming a battle with the sea. However, whatever planning you do, the most important skill is to pick up the messages the sea is giving and adapt your plan to suit what is happening to the kayak.

This chapter examines the planning and preparation that may prevent a simple sea kayak trip from becoming an epic.

PLANNING THE TRIP

> Navigation is the black art of knowing where you are while you are travelling from A to B.
> *Anon.*

'Passage planning' is the term 'salty sea dogs' use for the weather prediction and map/chart preparation done before going to sea. It can vary from simply finding out which way the tidal stream is flowing and when is the best time to start, to more complex plotting of estimated positions on a map/chart (dead reckoning).

Planning your journey requires a wide variety of questions to be answered, such as:

- Is the weather settled?
- Is the route safe?
- Are there any hazards?
- What navigation is needed?
- When is high and low water?
- How strong are the tidal streams?
- Is the kayak packed properly?

- Where is the wind blowing from?
- Where is the best place to land or camp?
- Is there a swell running?

... to name a few! If you tackle these questions methodically and thoroughly, you will be able to undertake your trip with confidence and get much more enjoyment from it.

During fine weather many kayak trips along the coast can be navigated by eye without in-depth chart plotting. You simply match the passing coastline to the map/chart and the only considerations are any weather changes, tidal currents and any hazards that may be met on the way. To neglect these, even on a simple sea trip, can, at the very least, mean that a lot more energy is expended fighting sea currents and at the worst an epic when the destination cannot be gained.

A longer trip or passage to an island off-shore may require more detailed planning of estimated positions after the tide has had its effect and drifted the kayak away from its destination. It is worth remembering to have an escape route and to carry the information needed to change the plan at sea.

Talk to People

Much of what sea paddlers do when planning a sea journey is gathering information and understanding how that information will hinder or help them. There is little point in starting to navigate until you can answer some questions, such as:

- Where do you want to go?
- What can you see on the way?
- Where to get on and off the water?
- Are you likely to encounter any ferries/ passenger boats on the way?
- Are there any dangers, such as overfalls?
- Will the paddle disturb wildlife?

Prior planning and preparation prevents a poor performance. Reading a chart before getting on the sea is a good idea.

- Is the trip protected from wind and swell?
- Is there anything interesting to visit on the way?

Extract local knowledge from other kayakers, fishermen and locals, but be discerning and ignore doom and gloom comments from those that believe everything is dangerous.

How Fast Do You Paddle?

An estimate of paddling speed allows you to plan a trip of a comfortable length for the experience of the paddlers. Unfortunately, this is not an exact science and will depend on the type of boat, fitness, load, aim of the trip, likely wind and sea conditions, and the capabilities of the paddlers.

It is most appropriate to measure the speed of a kayak in knots (kt), as tidal information is given in knots and the longitude and latitude scale on a sea chart are in nautical miles (nm): 1kt = 1nm/h, which is approximately 1.85km. A relative novice in a general purpose kayak in calm seas and light winds may paddle at 2–2.5kt, a leisurely pace in a sea kayak is 3–4kt, an unladen sea kayak is unlikely to go faster than 5–6kt over a short distance.

Wind Effect

The strength of the wind will also affect your paddling speed. Novices will experience difficulty paddling into a force 3, whereas experienced paddlers can cope with much more. It is obviously more efficient to paddle downwind, however, novices may find it difficult to keep their kayak in a straight line when there is a following sea (swell and wind from behind). Cross winds will drift the kayak sideways but by how much? To assess drift caused by the wind use a transit (*see* page 61). Although it is useful to estimate speed beforehand, to plan a trip it is more important to be able to calculate how fast the kayaks are moving at sea and to readjust timings (this will be covered later).

How Far Can You Paddle?

All of the elements affecting kayaking speed also affect kayaking distance. Most novices with improper paddling technique are exhausted after only a couple of miles. With proper technique and a moderate amount of practice, 13km (8 miles) in one day should be no problem. Intermediate paddlers should cope with 19–24km (12–15 miles) per day. Experienced paddlers should have no problem paddling 32km (20 miles) or more each day. Very fit and very experienced paddlers can go 64km (40 miles) a day. Occasionally you will hear stories of 128km (80 mile) days! Of course, sea state, wind, current direction and current strength have a lot to do with it. Catch the correct currents, and even a novice can paddle 22km (14 miles) in 3h.

There are several classic open crossings, which a number of paddlers aspire to: Lundy Island, the English Channel, the Irish Sea, St Kilda and so on. On such a paddle, a number of other factors can combine to make the journey far more hazardous. For example, a paddle from the Channel Islands to the closest point on the English mainland involves passing through two of the main tidal races along the coast of Britain. It also passes through some of the busiest shipping lanes in the world, is exposed to the westerly swell and the paddle is long enough in duration for quite considerable variations in the weather to occur. The decision to launch into a long, open crossing is one that requires careful consideration. The risks need to be weighed up and the decision made when you are in full receipt of all the information.

The Movement of the Sea (Tides and Tidal Streams)

The sea moves vertically (tides) and horizontally (tidal streams). It may surprise some people to know that all bodies of water move, including lakes, albeit with small movements. In the open ocean, tides are small (less than a metre), but when the ocean meets the land, tides become larger, especially when the sea is constricted by shallow sea beds, channels, bays and harbours.

Tides
In the UK there are two low and two high tides each day, caused by the gravitational pull of the moon and the sun, moving the water towards them. The sun is massive, but it is an average of 150 million km from the earth, compared with 384,400km for the moon. Since the moon is nearly 400 times closer to our planet, its influence on our oceans is almost twice as strong as the sun's. The period when the tides are coming in is called the flood and when they going out it is called the ebb. High waters are typically 12h 25min apart. The brief period between the flood and the ebb is called slack water. A common misconception is that slack water occurs both at high tide and low tide, but this is not always the case and local knowledge from Coastal Pilot books can help.

Because tides are accurately predicted we can plan and make corrections before the trip.

The Highest Tides

The highest tides in the world are found in the Bay of Fundy, Nova Scotia, Canada. At times during the year the difference between high and low tide may be as high as 16m (53ft), the equivalent of a three-storey building.

Reading Tide Tables

Tide tables give the times and heights above chart datum (theoretically the lowest possible tide) of high (HW) and low water (LW) for various standard ports (generally larger commercial ports), for example Dover for the south coast, Liverpool for the Irish Sea. A secondary port is a minor port or location such as the entrance to a river. Each is relative to a nearby standard port. Corrections for secondary ports can be found in Nautical Almanacs.

Tide times may need correcting for local changes such as: differences in time zone from universal time (UTC) and in countries operating daylight saving time in summer (constant: when the clocks go forward in spring add an hour, when they go back use the tables as they are). Some local tide tables are corrected for UT so take care reading them.

Time zone (UT)
For Summer Time add ONE
hour in non shaded areas

MAY

	Time	m		Time	m
1 W	0324	4.8	**16** TH	0404	5.0
	1004	0.9		1057	0.6
	1550	4.9		16.27	5.1
	2226	0.9		23.18	0.6
2 TH	0406	5.0	**17** F ●	0445	5.1
	1049	0.9		1139	0.5
	1630	5.0		1627	5.1
	2311	0.6		2359	0.6
3 F O	0447	5.1	**3** SAT	0523	5.0
	1133	0.5		1218	0.6
	1709	5.2		1739	5.1
	2353	0.5			

To find the time of HW or the height at a particular place, consult the tide tables at the nearest standard port. Then check the tables for the tidal difference for where the paddle is to take place (secondary port). For example, if HW occurs 20min later at the secondary port, then add 20 min.

The correction may be different for spring and neap tides; if you are in between neaps and springs, simply divide the difference in two.

However, plans do change, so carry information for recalculating at sea. Information about tides is found in Marine and Harbour Tide Tables, some newspapers, Reeds Nautical Almanac or from the coastguard. Coastal pilots are possibly the most useful source of tidal information because they give the changes close to shore where most sea paddlers play.

Tidal Range

The difference between high and low water is called the tidal range. It varies every day depending on the alignment of the sun and the moon. When they are in line they work together; therefore, at a new moon and fourteen days later at a full moon, the tidal range is at its greatest. These are called spring tides and they have higher high tides and lower low tides. The opposite occurs when the sun and the moon work against each other and the tidal movement is less. These are called neap tides, where the high tides are lower and the low tides higher. In fact the spring tides occur a few days after a new or full moon because it takes time to move the huge body of water. The time between spring and neap tides is approximately seven days. The tidal range and currents can increase by 50 per cent during spring tides! Each year there are twenty-six spring tides: thirteen at full moon and thirteen when the moon is a thin sliver of light.

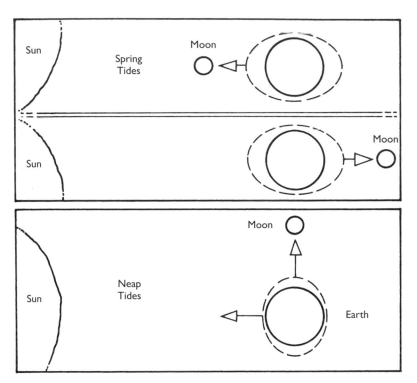

Neap and spring tides.

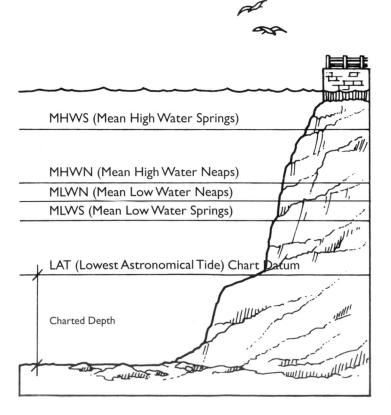

Tide heights.

The distance between the earth and the moon, and the earth and the sun, also varies as the moon rotates around the earth and the earth rotates around the sun. This means that the tidal range of the springs and neaps varies. The largest spring ranges occur near the solstices (21 June and 21 December); the weakest neap tides occur near the equinoxes (21 March and 23 September).

Meteorological conditions can also affect the tides and the accompanying tidal streams. A barometric pressure of 1,030 millibars depresses both low and high tides by 30cm (12in), whereas a pressure of 980 millibars allows levels to rise by 30cm. A strong onshore wind will increase the height of the tide and a strong offshore will decrease the height – tidal streams are affected accordingly. Whether it is high or low tide is usually only relevant to a sea kayaker because a low tide means a long carry up the beach, a carry through mud or a camp where the tents may be lost.

However, overfalls and sand bars produce some very turbulent seas at low tides, especially with the wind against the tide, and being able to work out depth at any moment is useful. The Rule of Twelfths is a simple arithmetical process for estimating the height of the tide between low and high water. If we assume the movement of the tide in and out to be a smooth symmetrical bell shape with a period of 12h, then the height changes over the full range in the 6h between HW and LW as follows:

- during first hour after HW the water drops $\frac{1}{12}$th of the full range;
- during the second hour an additional $\frac{2}{12}$th;
- during the third hour an additional $\frac{3}{12}$th;
- during the fourth hour an additional $\frac{3}{12}$th;
- during the fifth hour an additional $\frac{2}{12}$th;
- during the sixth hour an additional $\frac{1}{12}$th.

Hence, 2h after HW, the water has fallen $\frac{3}{12}$th of the full range. For example, when will the height of the tide at Shoreham reach 2.7m if LW is at 0735 1.0m, HW 1346 6.1m?

The range is 5.1m. To reach 2.7m tide needs to rise 1.7m, i.e. $\frac{1}{3}$ of the range.

This is $\frac{3}{12}$th of the range, therefore it will take 2h: $\frac{1}{12} + \frac{2}{12} + 20$min ($\frac{1}{3}$ of $\frac{3}{12}$).

The time is therefore 0955.

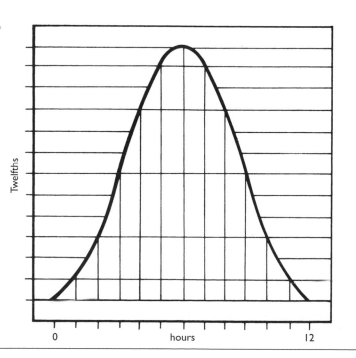

Rule of Twelfths

- Shape assumed to be sinusoidal
- Rise in $\frac{1}{12}$ths
  - 1 in first hour
  - 2 in second
  - 3 in third
  - 3 in fourth
  - 2 in fifth
  - 1 in sixth

Twelfths

0   hours   12

Tidal Flow

Tides are the vertical rise and fall of water, whereas tidal streams (a.k.a. tidal current) are the horizontal movement of water caused by the tides. Although the rise and fall of the tides can inconvenience a sea paddler (e.g. where to pitch a tent), what is more important is the direction and strength of the flow for the area and the time of the trip. Tidal streams are important because it is better to move with the tidal stream than against it, especially with spring tides when the tidal range is greatest and all that water still has to come fully in during the 6h interval. In the Faroe Islands, for example, the tidal streams can reach 12kt. Even an experienced sea paddler would find this impossible to fight against.

An important concept to grasp at this point is that the relationship between tide height and tidal currents is not simple. It does not follow that slack water occurs at high water and low water, in fact the water can continue to run out with the ebb even when the tide is still rising! Several factors contribute to this such as the momentum of the water, large bays storing water and differences in tide time along the coast. This has ramifications for sea paddlers

because the strongest portion of a tidal stream may be at high or low water depending on how the coastline affects the tidal streams, not when the tide is rising at its fastest as predicted by the rule of twelfths.

Where to Find the Speed and
Timing of Tidal Streams

Note: Tides are given for the direction they flow to, e.g. a northerly tide is flowing to the north. This is opposite to wind, where the direction is where the wind originates, e.g. a northerly wind comes from the north. There are four main sources.

TIDAL STREAM ATLASES

These can be bought or found in yachting almanacs and coastal pilots. Tidal stream atlases show the tidal currents for each hour of the tidal cycle. They comprise a total of twelve tidal charts ranging from 5h before HW until 6h after HW. These charts are therefore relative to the time of HW and to use them you need to know the absolute time of HW.

Though several layouts can be used, the direction of the tidal stream is usually shown by arrows, which are heavier where the tidal streams are stronger. Figures against the arrows give the mean neap and spring drift or rate in tenths of knots, e.g. 15,30 means the mean neap rate is 1.5kt and the spring 3.0kt. They are not much use for paddlers staying close to shore because they do not provide information about the effect the coast has on the flow.

CHART TIDAL DIAMONDS

These are the diamond-shaped symbols printed on admiralty charts (other chart publishers may use a circle rather than a diamond). Each diamond has a letter corresponding to a particular part of a data panel printed elsewhere on the chart (*see* diagram).

CHART TIDAL ARROWS

These give the mean rate. The arrow indicates the direction of flow. If the arrow has feathers, it indicates the direction of the flood tide (not the rate) and without, the ebb.

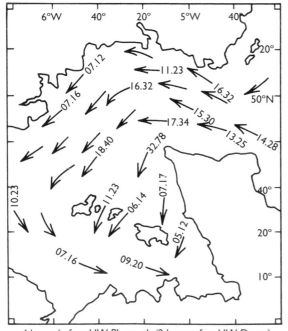

4 hours before HW Plymouth (2 hours after HW Dover)

An excerpt from a tidal stream atlas.

Sp 1.7 Np 0.9

———————————————▶ Direction of flood

◀———————————————

Tidal diamonds.

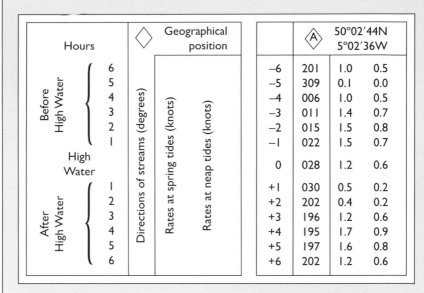

Hours		◇ Geographical position		Ⓐ 50°02′44N 5°02′36W		
Before High Water	6	Directions of streams (degrees)	Rates at spring tides (knots)	Rates at neap tides (knots)		
	5				−6	201	1.0	0.5

Directions are given from true north so a 90 stream flows eastwards. To calculate compass direction for the stream add mag variation. Be very careful when interpolating data from between two diamonds.

LOCAL PILOT BOOKS

These are probably the best source of tidal stream information as they have detailed local information on the movement of the streams close inshore and indicate any rough water.

What to Do When Detailed Information is Not Available

When information is not available, the fact that most tidal streams increase and decrease at a regular rate, allows paddlers to use the rule of thirds to estimate how far the tide would move them.

- After slack water, the tidal stream increases to reach its peak after 3h.
- From the previous information about tidal streams, neap tides are slower than spring tides. Take the information from the tidal stream atlas example given previously: Springs run at 3kt and neaps at 1.5kt. If you are in between neaps and springs, the rate is 2.25kt. Lets say that the pilot book has given springs with a peak flow of 3kt, the rule of thirds states:
  - during the first hour after the tide turns, the flow is moving at ⅓ its maximum, i.e. 1kt, therefore you will drift 1nm;

  - during the second hour after the tide turns, the tidal stream is running at ⅔ of its peak rate, i.e. 2kt, therefore you will drift 2nm;
  - during the third hour after the tide turns, it is running at its peak rate, i.e. 3kt, therefore you will drift 3nm;
  - during the fourth hour after the tide turns, it is still running at its peak rate, i.e. 3kt, therefore you will drift 3nm;
  - during the fifth hour after the tide turns, the tidal stream is running again at ⅔ of its peak rate, i.e. 2kt, therefore you will drift 2nm;
  - during the final, sixth hour after the tide turns, it decreases to ⅓ again, therefore you will drift 1nm;
- In some cases the tide runs for longer in one direction than the other and the rule must be adjusted accordingly. Shorter or longer time periods than 1h should then be used for the rule to work.

'Guestimating' Tidal Flow

It is important for paddlers to be able to interpolate the information to the area they are going to paddle. When there is no information, draw flow lines along the predicted direction and guess the tidal flow. Here are a few things to consider:

- Currents often flow parallel to shorelines.
- Confined waterways will cause the water to speed up, the narrower the channel the more it speeds up.
- The current in shallow water along a shore-line will be slower than the current in deeper off-shore water.
- Due to centrifugal force, the current along the outside edge of a smooth shoreline (concave shoreline) is faster than on the inside edge (convex shoreline) but of course the distance is greater to paddle – which course to take will depend on whether you are paddling into the wind; if you are, take the inside turn.
- Back eddies develop in bays downstream of points protruding into the sea. These can continue even after the main stream has changed direction. This can create eddy lines between the two moving bodies of water.
- When a waterway changes from flood to ebb, the current usually changes direction first in the shallow waters along its edge.
- Current flow often follows the path of the deepest water and will follow the contours of the sea-bed, not necessarily the shoreline.

Tidal Race

A tidal race is a localized region of fast, turbu-lent water with steep waves that occurs when-ever the flow of a strong current is abruptly altered by the land, such as a headland, or by the sea bed, such as sandbanks. They are sometimes shown on charts, but the ones that affect coastal paddlers are not often shown because they are too close to shore. Overfalls are related to tidal rips and occur when one current falls over another, commonly caused by headlands projecting out to sea under the water. Tidal races are affected by the wind strength and direction. When they are opposed, it can push the waves higher – this is known as wind against tide.

MAPS AND NAUTICAL CHARTS

Put a map on a boat and it becomes a chart, well almost. Charts are a map of the sea and only show land details that are visible from the sea. For the majority of sea trips, charts are not necessary and in fact a land map is often more useful. The advantage of a map is that it has a scale of 1:25,000 and shows more coastal features and shoreline details; their disadvantage is that they do not contain any navigational information such as buoys, lights and other features of the sea below low water – but this can be easily transferred from a chart to your map.

During the fifteenth century, mariners relied on charts called 'portalans'. They were simply centuries of seafarers' observations. As seafarers' skills improved and the compass became wide-spread, so did accuracy. Today we have charts that are absolutely accurate – but only on the day they were produced! Charts change as sand and mud move about, buoys are moved and so on. Charts can be updated with these changes using information contained in Notices to Mariners published weekly. Presently there are three suppliers of charts in the UK: Admiralty, Imray and Stanford. In the USA they are produced by the National Ocean Service (*see* Appendix for information on where to obtain charts).

Scale

Maps and charts are produced in a wide range of scales. The scale of a chart is the relationship between the distance of two points on a chart and the two points in the real world. This rela-tionship is usually referred to by a ratio such as 1:40,000. This means that 1in on the chart equals 40,000in in the real world. Small scale, small detail; large scale, large detail.

A small-scale chart is one that represents objects smaller than in a larger scale chart, but it can represent a larger portion of the earth. A 1:40,000-scale chart is therefore a smaller scale chart than a 1:20,000-scale chart. Harbour and other local charts are generally large scale (1:5,000 and 1:25,000), while off-shore charts are generally smaller scale (1:75,000 to 1:3,500,000). Maps come in a variety of scales, the most useful for sea paddling is the 1:25,000.

Map and Chart Projections

Charts (and maps) are a flat representation of part of the earth's spherical surface. The process of flattening a sphere creates distortion that is further exaggerated because the earth is not a smooth sphere (the circumference between the poles is smaller than around the equator). With a few exceptions at high latitudes, the most

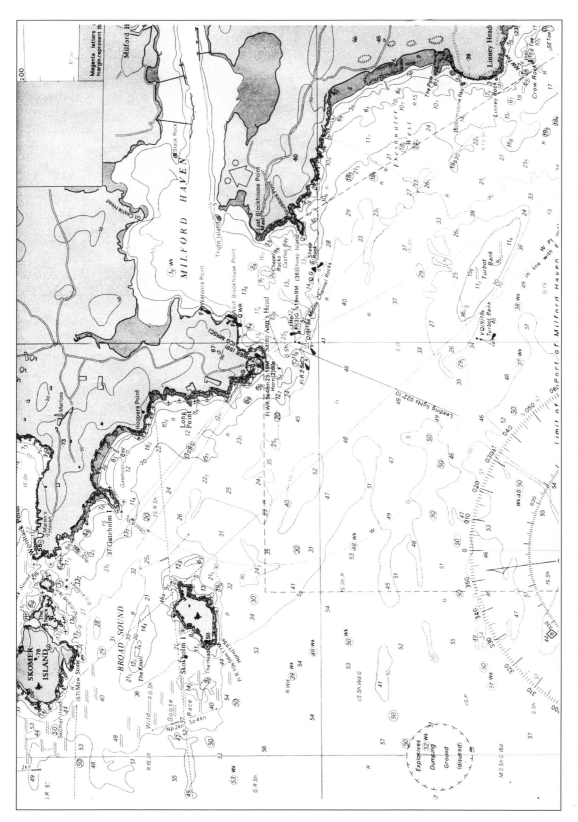

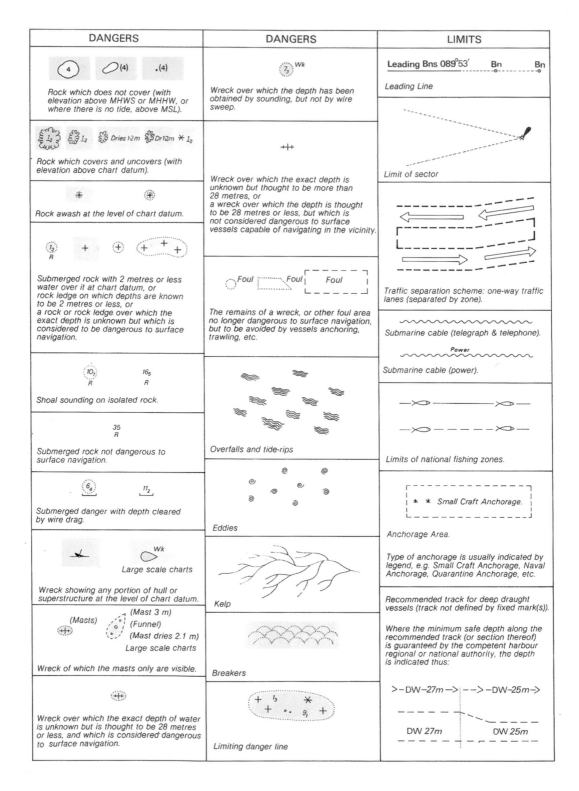

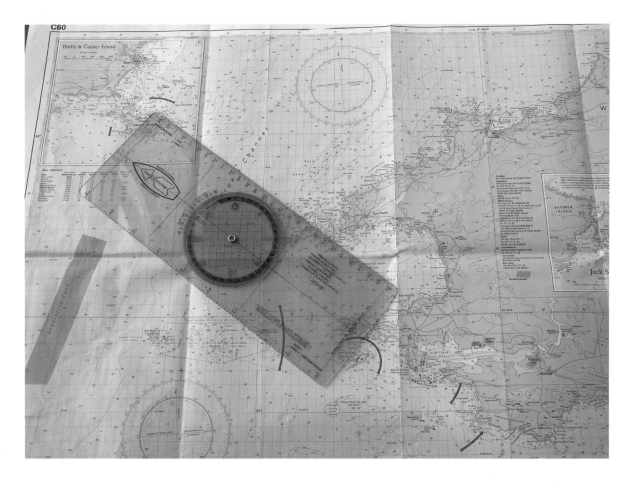

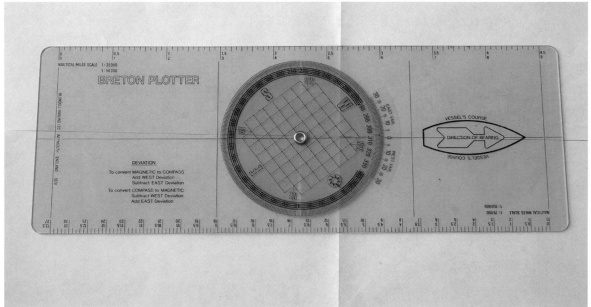

A Breton chart plotter.

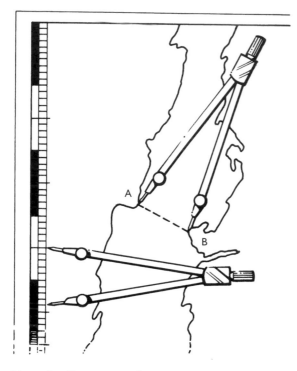

Measuring distance on a chart.

common chart that paddlers will use is based on the 'Mercator' projection, after Gerard Kremer in 1569. He wrapped a cylinder around a globe so that it touched the equator and then projected the surface features of the earth onto it. Nowadays it is mathematically calculated. The Mercator projection causes the longitude lines (meridians) to converge as they move northwards or southwards – they are not really parallel, they only appear to be on large-scale charts. Because of this distortion, only the latitude lines are used for measuring distance, except at the equator where longitude can also be used. The Mercator projection is the reason why most school children believe that the UK is almost the same size as Africa, and Greenland is shown almost as big as North America. This distortion is not usually a problem for sea paddlers because the scale of charts represent such a small part of the world.

What Information Does a Chart Contain?

A chart has information such as places of interest, tide races, overfalls, eddies, landing spots and their likely character, lights, buoys and shape and depth of the sea bed and other prominent features, shoreline character and so on. The main reason for knowing the system of buoys and lights is to be able to stay out of the way of big shipping that travels along set channels.

- Depths: a sounding, e.g. 35, indicates 3.5m (11ft) of water above chart datum. An underlined sounding indicates an object that shows above the LAT.
- Isobaths/depth contours: lines connecting positions of the same depth.
- Heights: lighthouses, mountains and cliffs are shown relative to mean high water spring (MHWS).
- Tidal information: details of the horizontal and vertical movement of the water.
- Buoys and markers: lightships, lateral, cardinal markers.
- Sea bed qualities: pebbles, seaweed, rocks, wrecks, pipelines and so on.
- Magnetic variation: this is indicated in the compass rose.
- Conspicuous positions on shore: churches, radio masts, mountain tops that can be used for navigation are shown.

Compass Rose

Charts have a compass called a compass rose drawn onto the map. This compass is corrected for magnetic variation, i.e. north points to magnetic north, but only for the date of publication.

Latitude and Longitude

In order to be able to describe a particular point on the earth, we need an artificial grid (co-ordinate) system to describe the spot. Remember the board game 'Battleships'? That grid system used letters to describe the vertical plane, and numbers to describe the horizontal. In real-world navigating we use latitude and longitude for our grids.

Latitude
The world is roughly a sphere, about 21,638nm in diameter at the equator. Imagine a dot on the top and another at the bottom that represent the north and south poles. Now draw a line completely around the waist of the sphere dividing it in half, this is the equator. Continue drawing

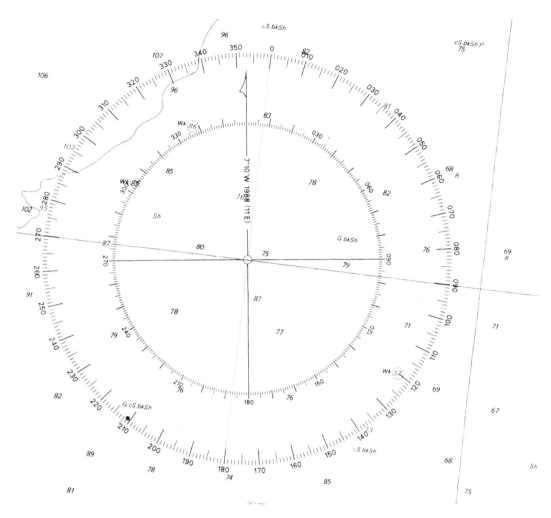

Compass rose. © Crown Copyright and/or database rights. Reproduced by permission of the Controller of Her Majesty's Stationery Office and the UK Hydrographic Office (www.ukho.gov.uk).

circles parallel to the equator but towards each pole. These are parallels of latitude. Each parallel of latitude specifies a point on the vertical plane even though they are horizontal. Each parallel is named with the number of degrees it represents from the equator (which is 0 degrees): the north pole is 90 degrees north. All parallels above the equator and within the northern hemisphere are labelled north. South of the equator we begin again at zero, continuing to the south pole which is 90 degrees south.

A degree of latitude is divided into sixty minutes. Each minute is divided into sixty seconds. One minute of latitude (1′) is equal to 1 nautical mile, therefore it is 90 degrees of latitude from the equator to the north pole. So the distance from the equator to the north pole equals 5,400nm.

Longitude
Draw circles around the sphere but this time with each circle going through each pole. These are called meridians of longitude. The first or prime meridian (zero) of longitude runs through the British Royal Observatory in Greenwich. Meridians are labelled from 0 to 180 degrees going east and west: 180 degrees is on the opposite side of the world from Greenwich. So meridians are imaginary circles around the earth that converge at both poles.

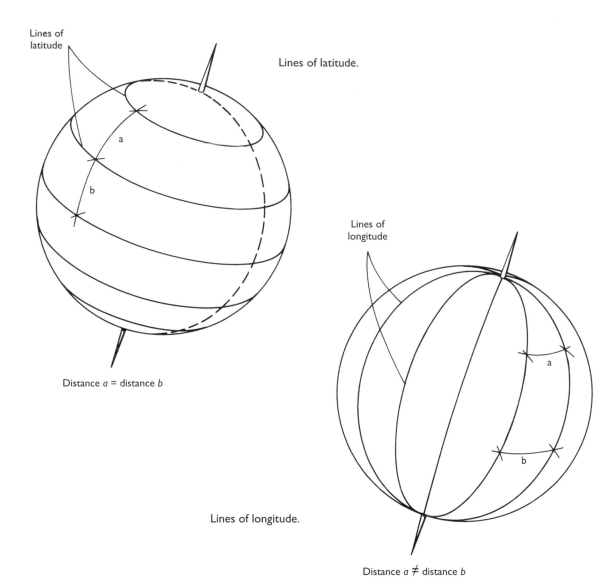

Lines of latitude.

Distance *a* = distance *b*

Lines of longitude.

Distance *a* ≠ distance *b*

Note: Meridians of longitude are not parallel to each other as lines of latitude are. Meridians are considered great circles. A great circle is a circle drawn around the earth that, if the earth were sliced along it, would slice through the centre core of the earth. Parallels of latitude are not great circles, except for one – the equator.

CHARTWORK

Combining the information gained from charts, tide tables and pilots with the aims and objectives of the journey, the sea paddler can plan a trip that is achievable, safe and challenging.

'Waypoints' and Measuring Distance

Exact position at sea is only truly known at the start and finish of the trip, the rest of the time your position may be suspect. Plotting a course and marking where the kayak is likely to travel is called 'dead reckoning'. It is not often that a kayaker has to resort to pure dead reckoning without any landmarks. After deciding where the paddle is to be, plot points that will be passed on the way ('waypoints'), measure the distance, calculate the magnetic bearing using a course plotter (see below) between the points and write the information on the chart or map. To measure distance use dividers or a piece of string. Open the dividers between the 'waypoints' and match the dividers with the latitude scale on the edge of the chart. It is incorrect to use the longitude scale because the meridians converge as you go northwards or southwards. The only place on a longitude scale where 1 nautical mile equals one minute is at the equator.

1′ (latitude) = 1nm.
1 degree = 60′ or 60nm.
1nm = 1,852m (6,074ft).

These waypoints are obviously estimations of where you would like to be, but they are only going to apply when there is no tidal or wind effects on the kayak. A later section looks at how to plot corrections for tidal effects.

Using the Tidal Information

When the tidal stream is very small, it can be ignored and the magnetic bearing for that leg

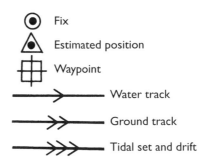

There are standard symbols used for plotting on a chart.

calculated using the compass rose on the chart or a chart plotter (allow for variation: *see* Chapter 6) and simply paddle along it.

The tide can be used in a number of ways to assist the paddler:

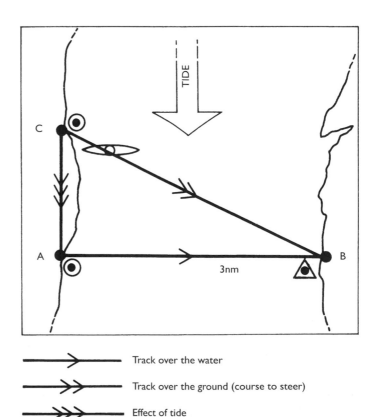

Starting further up the coast to use the tide:

- the tidal flow is 5kt, i.e. 5nm/h for 1h;
- the crossing A–B distance is 3nm;
- assume paddling at 3nm/h;
- then simply start at point C 5nm further up the coast, the tide will push you down towards the island.

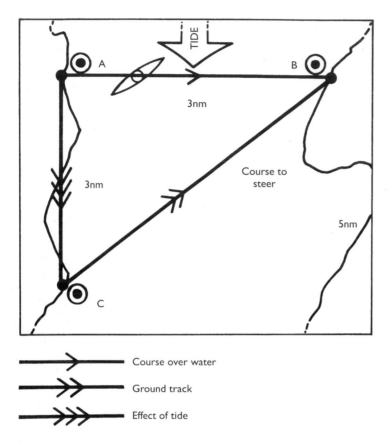

Course over water

Ground track

Effect of tide

Plotting the effects of a tidal stream on a short crossing A to B:

- A is the start point;
- given that average paddling speed is 3nm/h, calculate how long it would take to paddle from A to B. Another 1hr;
- draw line A – C to represent how far a 3nm/hr tide would drift an unattended kayak for 1 hour (the time taken to paddle from A to B);
- join C to B – this is the direction (course to steer) you should paddle your kayak to counteract the tide;
- use a chart plotter to find the bearing and correct for variation.

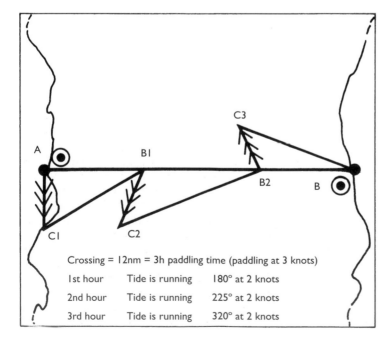

Crossing = 12nm = 3h paddling time (paddling at 3 knots)

1st hour	Tide is running	180° at 2 knots
2nd hour	Tide is running	225° at 2 knots
3rd hour	Tide is running	320° at 2 knots

Using tidal triangles on a long passage:

- assume point A is the start;
- given your average paddling speed, calculate how long it would take to paddle from point A to point B1;
- draw the line A–C to scale for the first leg (then B–C) in the direction of the tidal stream, to represent the distance and direction a kayak would drift if unattended for the time it would take to paddle each leg;
- join C1–B1, then C2–B2, then C3–B3: these will be the courses to paddle for each leg;
- transfer it across to the compass rose or use a chart plotter to find the bearing, allow for variation, then write the bearing and distance.
- this is a very long-winded method: it is probably better to add and subtract the tidal effect over the whole distance to give a final course to steer.

- Plan the start or return time to use the tidal flow to help rather than hinder the trip.
- On a crossing to an island start further up the coast and use the tide to drift towards the target (*see* diagram).
- If the crossing is short (less than 30min), travel at slack water.
- If the tidal stream flows at the same rate in both directions, time the crossing so that the tide pushes the kayak in one direction for the first half of the trip and the other direction for the second half.

Any method for calculating the effect the tide will have on a kayak is only an estimation; it is important to examine the chart and find any obvious features and transit lines along the way and note them on the map or scribble sheet. This will save time when at sea. Note any light characteristics, particularly for legs towards the end of the day, in case you get caught out in the dark.

When the tidal stream is significant it may be necessary to find out how much the tide is going to drift the kayak by creating a tidal triangle. This is called dead reckoning, i.e. reckoning where the kayak will be after a set time of paddling after the effects of tides are taken into account. If the tidal flow direction changes during the crossing, simply plot the tidal changes for the new leg.

On large, open crossings it may be necessary to split the crossing into smaller legs of a few hours' paddling and construct a new tidal triangle for each leg as the tidal stream changes.

NAVIGATION AT SEA

Setting Up a Kayak for a Sea Trip

The first problem that a sea paddler faces when navigating at sea is that spray decks make poor chart tables, meaning that navigation techniques are best preplanned and kept as simple as possible. Plus, if you let go of a tool or chart it is likely to go overboard; roll and everything is soaked or lost. Standard navigation tools, such as parallel rulers, chart plotters and dividers, are designed for warm, dry navigation stations. Therefore plotting a course once at sea is generally a non-event in a kayak and navigation should be based on predetermined compass bearings on which the boat can be lined up, or definite and visible transits (points of reference)

An example navigation set-up on a sea kayak.

that do not require the use of a compass or chart plotting. Tools that work aboard a kayak have to be small, durable and water resistant, for instance a piece of string instead of a pair of dividers. Another limitation to navigating from a kayak is the close horizon created by its low vantage point. This problem is made worse when the sea is rough, obscuring easily identifiable places and objects on a featureless shoreline, such as the mouth of a river or beach.

Maps and charts are printed on paper and, when they get wet (which they will), they become costly mush. Waterproofing them goes a long way toward helping them survive immersion and subsequent mildew. A good way is to laminate sections of the map/chart using 'Fablon' (sticky backed plastic), but remember that the section that you are using may lack important things like the compass rose, tidal diamonds and the scale. So, before water-proofing a map/chart, it is a good idea to photo-copy these and add another compass rose (see-through ones can be purchased to put on the chart). Some care is needed to make sure that the rose is lined up so that north is in line with magnetic north and does not obscure key navigational information. Before waterproofing, consider whether to write any useful notes on the chart and to add a scale or two.

The important thing is to keep tools to hand. Mount the waterproofed chart, with the first few legs visible, on the foredeck of the kayak. Charts are best secured by putting them in a trans-parent case, even when waterproofed. Do not depend just on the deck bungies to hold the case securely, use a case with clips. The smaller the chart case, the more times the chart must be folded, so use the biggest chart case that will fit on the deck without hanging over the side. Notes (course details and so on) are generally written on a white piece of self-adhesive plastic on deck.

Besides charts, tools to measure bearing and distance may be required. Most of the standard devices for figuring distance/direction on a chart are too complex for use on the deck of a kayak. Kayak navigation is an art, not a science so, to be artful, try using hands as tools. Try various finger joints, finger extensions, finger widths and hand spans against the scale on the chart. There is always something that is close to a nautical mile or a kilometre, and something that is close to 5 nautical miles.

A serious sea paddler will require a deck-mounted compass and a hand-held compass to take bearings on land objects rather than turning the kayak to line the front of the boat up on the object. The compass should be carefully mounted away from metal objects for obvious reasons.

Direction at Sea

The sea is a moving body of water and direction can mean many things. There are a number of terms that need explaining:

- bearing is the direction of one object from another;
- course is the direction the kayak is intended to travel whether that be sideways or not;
- heading is the direction the bow of the kayak is pointing at any given moment;
- track is the direction the kayak moves over the surface of the earth.

Birds can do it, whales, butterflies and pigeons can too, but unfortunately humans are not so clever; just try paddling on a set course in the mist without a compass – the route travelled will more than likely resemble a circle. The compass provides the ability to consistently steer the kayak on a course or to find direction to a distant object. A compass is simply a fluid-filled container with a magnetized needle rotating on a pivot that aligns itself with magnetic north and south. Luckily, the earth has a magnetic field that is roughly aligned with the north and south poles. Unfortunately magnetic north and south are not true north and south, the difference is called magnetic variation. The north magnetic pole is situated approximately 78.9 N latitude and 103.8 W, 960km (600 miles) from the true north pole. Therefore the compass will point to a direction other than true north; the difference is called variation (declination), the value of which will depend where you are in relation to magnetic north. Some places have no variation, whereas others have extreme magnetic variation. Therefore, a compass bearing taken from the chart or map must be corrected by adding the variation from true north (this information will be found on the chart or map). The compass rose will have the magnetic variation for that chart contained on it, but remember it is not constant – the magnetic pole migrates, so check the chart date and the annual increase or decrease in variation written inside the compass rose.

There are a number of ways of determining direction from a chart: a pair of parallel rules or a specialized protractor called a course plotter are the most widely used (I highly recommend the latter for ease of use). A course plotter is basically a clear plastic straight edge with a protractor and a parallel ruler is two rulers linked together, which allows them to be walked across the page to the compass rose.

By the time the trip has started the passage will have been planned, points plotted on the map, the effects of tide estimated and the course corrected, the weather checked, dangers high-lighted, compass bearing plotted, possible tran-sits highlighted, notable sights on the way, and points that can be used to confirm position.

Funnily enough a sea paddle rarely goes to plan, many things affect the planned route that

A three-point fix to pinpoint position.

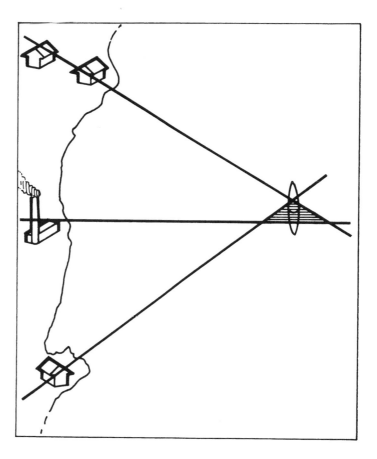

cannot be allowed for on land, such as the effect of the wind, a change in paddling speed, sickness, injury, atmospheric pressure and wind affecting the tides and creating waves. All of these things may change the passage prepared on land and the sea paddler will have to adapt the chosen route or do something to stay on it. Pay attention to position and update it on the chart as often as possible, especially if fog or mist are around.

Confirming Position at Sea

The course the kayak takes may be affected by the wind or the sea state and therefore may be completely different from the bearings plotted while still on land. When the conditions allow, check for sideways movement of the kayak. To do this use cross-bearings and/or transits.

Single-point fix: the best fix is to pass close to something obvious like a headland or buoy that is shown on the chart.

Three-point fix: this is simply taking a bearing on three well-spaced objects on land, identifying them on the chart and drawing a line from the object that follows the bearing (do not forget to remove magnetic variation before plotting on the chart). Once the three lines are drawn, the intersection is the kayak's position. It is more likely that the three lines will produce a triangle (a cocked hat); the kayak is somewhere inside the triangle, so hopefully your triangle is not too large.

Transits or ranges: a transit or range is any two points that line up. Because transit lines require no instruments to be used, they are very accurate. Simply identify two object on land that are in line, identify them on the chart and draw a line through them. Your position is somewhere on that line. If the process is repeated on another two objects, position can be found. The advantage of transits is that they provide immediate feedback as to the progress of the kayak and whether there is any drift due to the influence of either the wind or tide.

The technique is simple but effective. Select two stationary objects, which are some distance apart, and observe how they move in relation to one another. If the two objects remain in line then the paddler is still on course. If the rear object moves to the right of the nearest object, then you are being carried to the right of your course. If the rear object moves to the left, then you are being carried to the left of your course.

Transits can provide constant feedback as to how the wind or tidal streams are affecting the kayak. The boat can be used as an extended direction of travel arrow when taking cross-bearings or transits using the compass fitted to the deck. Aim the bow of the kayak at a fixed point whenever possible and paddle towards that rather than paddling on a compass bearing. For taking bearings, it is easier to use a Silva land compass than to manoeuvre the boat to allow the deck-mounted compass to be used; plus it is also there as a backup and for use on land.

Measuring Speed at Sea

This can be done simply by measuring the time it takes to travel between two objects. This does not necessarily indicate how fast the paddler is paddling but how fast the boat is moving relative to the two objects; this is because the speed of the kayak is the addition of the paddling speed plus or minus the speed of the tidal current and any effect of wind.

How Far Away is an Object or Land

Using one of the methods for fixing position outlined above will tell you where you are, it is

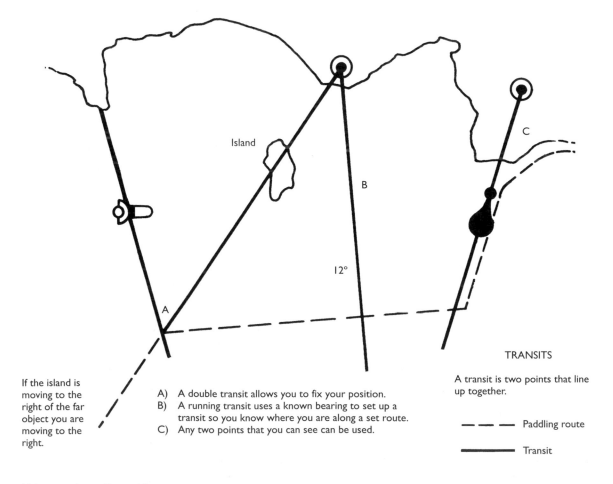

Island

C

B

12°

A

TRANSITS

A transit is two points that line up together.

If the island is moving to the right of the far object you are moving to the right.

A) A double transit allows you to fix your position.
B) A running transit uses a known bearing to set up a transit so you know where you are along a set route.
C) Any two points that you can see can be used.

– – – – Paddling route

———— Transit

Using transits to fix position.

then a simple case of measuring on the map how far away the object is. You can estimate the distance by using the following as a guide:

- at 8km (5 miles), large houses, towers and ships can be seen by the naked eye;
- at 3km (2 miles), large trees and windows on houses can be seen;
- at 1.5km (1 mile), large buoys can be seen;
- at ½ mile people appear as dots;
- at 0.5km (¼ mile), hands, arms and paddle blades can be seen;
- at 0.25km (⅛ mile) faces, etc., can be seen.

You can also measure a section of shoreline and use that to judge the distance to an object.

Using a Global Positioning System (GPS)

GPS is a satellite-based navigation system devised by the USA military and still remains under military control. As a consequence of a Korean airliner being destroyed when it wandered into Soviet air space, the system was made accessible to civilians. GPS gives you latitude and longitude co-ordinates anywhere on the earth and in any weather. It can also give direction, the speed moving over the sea, distance to a location and even altitude.

GPS receivers look like mobile phones. Waterproof GPS units are becoming more affordable but a waterproof bag adds security and flotation. Most GPS units will drain batteries in about 12h, so carry spare batteries and only turn it on when needed. To communicate with satellites they must be placed on the deck with the antenna vertical to work properly. The detailed working of a GPS is beyond the scope of this book and the instruction manual for each model should be examined carefully to get the best from them.

Position is given in latitude and longitude to the nearest ¹⁄₁₀₀th of a minute – it can give your position to within a few kayak lengths! The operational accuracy of GPS is, however, not constant – it is a military system and they control it using something called selective availability (SA), which can vary between 100m and 20m. The problem is we do not know what it is at any given time or place. One solution is to use a differential GPS, independent of SA, that co-ordinates signals from satellites with land-based signals from known locations.

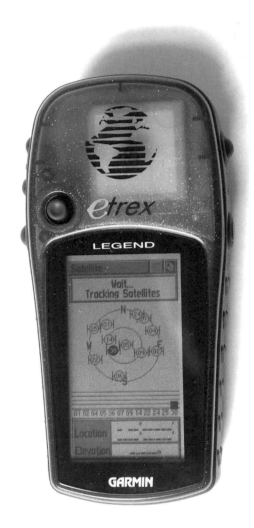

A GPS unit.

Chart Datums

Having said all that, you would think that any fixed point on the earth's surface would have just one latitude and one longitude to describe where it is. Sadly this is not the case. An analogy that explains why datums change is to get two sheets of A4 paper, line them up exactly and with the tip of your pencil punch a small hole through both sheets. Give one sheet to a helper and ask them to divide the page into squares by ruling vertical and horizontal lines on it. You do the same with your sheet. Then ask them to tell you how many horizontal lines up from the bottom and how many vertical lines in from the left edge their punched hole is. Your helper's punched hole will be a different number of lines up from the bottom and in from the edge than yours because you each drew your vertical and horizontal lines with different spacings. The hole is in exactly the same place on the sheet of paper, but you each describe it as being in a different place depending on how you have divided your page into squares. You both have different datums.

Replace the piece of paper with the earth's surface and there are literally hundreds of different datums in use to record the position of a point on it. Different countries have their own datums in which their country is mapped and if you have a GPS unit there are dozens of selectable datums preloaded into it so that the unit can be used anywhere in the world to match up with the maps and charts produced in that country to the county's own datum. If you are using your GPS unit in Australia, for instance, you will need to set it to the Australian ADG66 or ADG84 datum to match Australian-produced maps and charts; if you are in the USA, you would probably be using maps and charts in the NAD83 or NAD27 datum to which your GPS unit must be set to match up with them. In the UK, most maps and charts are in Ordnance Survey (OS) datum and in order to match your GPS unit to OS maps you would have to set it to OS datum.

There is a light at the end of this tunnel, however. In 1984 a world geodetic survey was published and it is now possible to produce maps and charts of the earth's surface to one common datum, which is abbreviated to WGS84. Many countries are in the process of converting their country's maps and charts to WGS84 datum, and the UK Admiralty have embarked on doing this for UK maritime charts, which are currently in the OS datum. The trouble is that at the moment we are in an interim situation with some charts and maps being in local datums and some in the common WGS84 datum. It is therefore necessary to be very careful how you use paper maps and charts with your GPS unit, because the difference between different datums can be as much as several hundreds of metres, which at sea could be disastrous in terms of navigation

Speed Over the Ground and
Course Over the Ground
A GPS has another use: it can tell where the kayak is actually going rather than the bearing it is on. The kayak may be following a bearing, but

---

Top Tip

It may seem that GPS takes all the hard work and skill out of navigation but they are electronic pieces of equipment and do fail to work at times. Do not depend on a GPS alone – a boat compass is still needed to maintain a course. Plus they eat batteries so using the GPS as a compass is expensive.

---

the actual direction it is moving in may be different. You may be paddling north at 2kt with a tidal stream running north at 2kt. Speed over the ground (SOG) is therefore 4kt and the course over the ground (COG) will be the same as the compass bearing. However, if you were paddling due north at 2kt and the tidal flow was NE at 2kt, the GPS would show a SOG of approximately 3.8 and a COG of 018. You are therefore not travelling where the compass is pointing because the tide is pushing you away from your intended track.

Using Waypoints
The biggest challenge in GPS use is transferring the position indicated in the unit to the chart/map. Plotting latitudes and longitudes at sea is difficult, instead preload waypoints (specific locations) that you have loaded into the GPS and marked on the chart. Since the GPS can use only a limited number of letters for a name assigned to a waypoint (that need remembering!) use a 3in by 5in waterproof notebook to record the names of the waypoints, and for other useful navigational data needed at sea, such as line-of-sight distances for various eye heights, rules of thumb, formulae and the like. In addition to the waterproof notebook, a soft pencil or a grease pencil to write things down on the deck or on something similar to the white plastic note board made for sea kayakers or scuba divers is useful.

There are two basic ways to use waypoints:

1. Call up the desired waypoint, read the course to it and head in that direction. Set the display to show COG and then watch how this compares to the desired course. If you are in a tidal flow, the compass bearing and COG will not agree and the course paddled must be changed.

2. Choose not only a destination waypoint but also a departure waypoint from which the GPS will choose the straight line between them. You can then guide your kayak along that line and forget the actual way your kayak is pointing. This is called cross track error, i.e. how far off your intended route you are.

Please remember that using a GPS to paddle along a line will eat batteries!

Digital Maps

Charts and maps are also available in digital format on CD-ROM. The waterproof, integrated kayak computer navigation station is still in the future, so charts need to be printed at home. This is convenient because they are then single sheets and one is usually all that is needed for a short paddle. If more are needed, a small trip book can be created. The nice thing about printing charts is that one can be made for each person in the group, and they can be scaled to the required level of detail. Make sure that a distance scale is included on the printout.

If a GPS is used, it is possible to print tracks and data from a GPS onto the chart or map. With some programs the computer can be used to make it easy to load the GPS with waypoints. A computer with the appropriate navigation software makes it much easier to determine waypoints for the logbook and GPS while you are planning your trip. An alternative to locating position with cumbersome latitude and longitude readings, the GPS can calculate the direction and distance to the centre of the compass rose, a position that has been entered as a waypoint in the GPS. The GPS will give the distance and direction to the compass rose. With a piece of string scaled for kilometres (or miles) and the reciprocal bearing, position can then be easily found. Even if you do not invest in the full CD-ROM charts, most GPS manufacturers provide simple data-entry software that comes with a GPS-to-PC cord.

Paddling in Poor Visibility

There are times on the sea when we can get caught out by either advancing fog or darkness, in which case the paddler should make time to prepare themselves and the group. If on or near the land in a safe location, should the group consider landing and arranging a lift or should they move on? When caught out at sea the paddler should:

- ascertain their position as accurately as possible and work out the closest safe landing point;
- remove themselves from areas of shipping traffic;
- stow or secure loose kit and use a paddle leash;
- put into effect a suitable method of group control, e.g. numbering off, give each member of the group a number and occasionally ask them to repeat it: no number – no paddler;
- if possible contact any pre-arranged contacts to let them know you will be late back and give an ETA – this may prevent an unnecessary coastguard search.

CHAPTER 5

WEATHER, WIND AND THE SEA

The Sea at night can be a fright,
Like none you've ever seen.
There's monsters there that lurk beneath
That ghostly sub-marine.
Pirate's ships and Witches' slips
And treasures cursed to Hell!
It'd do you right to sleep at night
Than mind the foam and swell.

Lilian Alessa

WEATHER

An enthusiastic sea paddler will become obsessed with the weather because it rules when and where to go sea paddling. When we talk about weather what we are really discussing are the conditions in the atmosphere. A competent sea paddler should be able to:

- find the sources of information, including forecasts, and be able to interpret them;
- recognize the main pressure systems and the cloud, weather and wind patterns associated with them;
- understand how the weather affects the sea;
- appreciate the effect of local conditions in modifying forecasts;
- learn to blend theory with real life, e.g. how will an increase in pressure affect the party, will it be a 'head wind' or a 'tail wind'?

WHERE TO OBTAIN WEATHER INFORMATION

Information on weather is obtained from a number of sources, each has its pros and cons.

Television

The forecasts provided by TV stations vary tremendously. Sometimes they give you wind direction and sometimes they do not. They are often poor at showing what is happening to depressions (cyclones) out at sea that will determine the swell. The big disadvantage is that if you are distracted, important information can easily be missed.

Radio

The forecasts given on the radio again vary from absolutely useless to providing a lot of good information. Some local radio stations in popular sailing areas provide special forecasts for sailors and windsurfers. In the UK, the shipping forecast on Radio 4 is broadcast every six hours and includes general synopsis, forecasts for the different sea areas and reports of actual weather from selected stations. They provide good background information but they are not very specific and you need to concentrate and avoid distraction to get the best from them.

Shipping Forecasts and Inshore Waters Forecasts

The Met Office creates the shipping forecasts/ bulletins that are broadcast on BBC Radio 4.

UK Shipping Forecast Areas
Weather bulletins for shipping are broadcast daily on BBC Radio 4 at the following times: 0048 and 0535 (long wave and FM), 1200 and 1755 (normally long wave only). The bulletins consist of a gale warning summary, general synopsis, sea-area forecasts and coastal station reports. In addition, gale warnings are broadcast at the first available programme break after

Wind Direction
Wind direction indicates the direction from which the wind is blowing not to where it is blowing.

A big sea in Pembrokeshire. The cliffs are 60m (200ft) high!

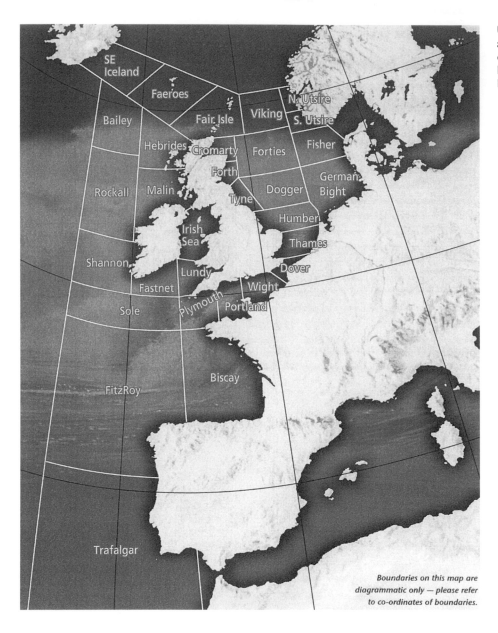

UK shipping forecast
areas. © Crown
copyright 2006.
Published by the
Met. Office.

*Boundaries on this map are
diagrammatic only — please refer
to co-ordinates of boundaries.*

receipt. If this does not coincide with a news
bulletin, the warning will be repeated after the
next news bulletin.

Glossary of Shipping Bulletin Terms
Gale warnings:

- gale – winds of at least Beaufort force 8
  (34–40kt) or gusts reaching 43–51kt;
- severe gale – winds of force 9 (41–47kt) or
  gusts reaching 52–60kt;

- storm – winds of force 10 (48–55kt) or gusts
  reaching 61–68kt;
- violent storm – winds of force 11 (56–63kt)
  or gusts of 69kt or more;
- hurricane force – winds of force 12 (64kt or
  more).

Note: The term used is 'hurricane force'; the
term 'hurricane' on its own means a true
tropical cyclone, not experienced in British
waters.

Map of Met. Office inshore
waters forecast. © Crown
copyright 2006. Published by
the Met. Office.

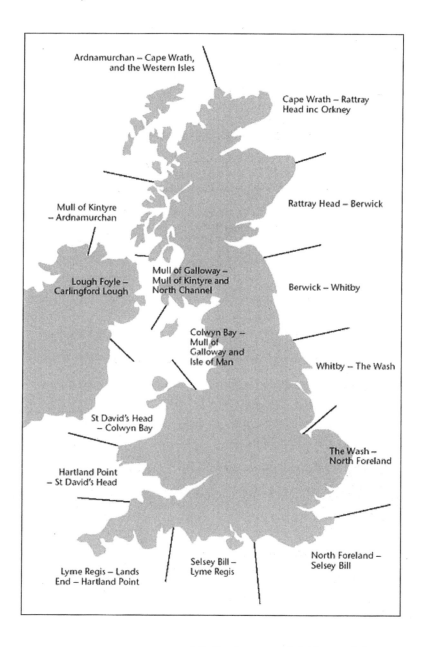

Timing:

- imminent – expected within 6h of time of issue;
- soon – expected within 6–12h of time of issue;
- later – expected more than 12h from time of issue.

Visibility:

- fog – visibility less than 1,000m;
- poor – visibility between 1,000m and 2nm;
- moderate – visibility between 2 and 5nm;
- good – visibility more than 5nm.

Movement of pressure systems:

- slowly – moving at less than 15kt;
- steadily – moving at 15–25kt;
- rather quickly – moving at 25–35kt;
- rapidly – moving at 35–45kt;
- very rapidly – moving at more than 45kt.

Storm clouds over the Pembrokeshire coast.

Pressure tendency in station reports:

- rising (or falling) slowly – pressure change of 0.1–1.5mb in the preceding 3h;
- rising (or falling) – pressure change of 1.6–3.5mb in the preceding 3h;
- rising (or falling) quickly – pressure change of 3.6–6.0mb in the preceding 3h;
- rising (or falling) very rapidly – pressure change of more than 6.0mb in the preceding 3h;

- now rising (or falling) – pressure has been falling (rising) or steady in the preceding 3h, but at the time of observation was definitely rising (falling).

Forecasts for Inshore Waters
In addition, some bulletins include a forecast for all UK inshore waters, as distinct from the coastal waters. This can be heard on BBC Radio 4 at the end of programmes (approximately 0048), and on BBC Radio 3 at 0535. The

forecast covers the area up to 19km (12 miles) off-shore and is for the period up to 1800 the next day. It includes a general synopsis, the forecast of wind direction and force, visibility and weather. The broadcast on Radio 4 also includes the latest available reports of wind direction and force, visibility, sea-level pressure and tendency for approximately twenty stations around the UK.

Newspapers

Weather maps are a great way to obtain information but they do need interpretation. They are often out of date when compared with other sources of information. The advantage is that you can take it with you and read it at your leisure.

Local Coastguard Stations

For local immediate information on what is happening at sea they can be great. If you have a VHF radio you can listen to the coastguard for information on the weather (refer to the local almanac for channels and times).

Internet

This is a great way to obtain weather information because you can take your time and it can be printed out (*see* Appendix for web sites).

UNDERSTANDING WEATHER

The weather is a constant topic of conversation amongst those who paddle on the sea, especially in the temperate regions of the world, because here great air masses of different temperatures, pressures and moisture content fight for supremacy.

The energy to drive the world's weather comes from the sun, and because of the angle of the earth to the sun, the world is warmed unevenly. Warm air rises and is replaced by cold air, rather like a bonfire. Therefore air at the equator rises and is replaced by colder air moving in from elsewhere. As the air flows from the poles towards the equator it is deflected to the west and air moving from the equator is deflected to the east, by the spinning of the earth. This is the Coriolis effect – imagine a person standing on the north pole: they are spinning, however, at the equator they are not spinning but moving with the earth. Combining this with the fact that air moves from areas of high pressure to areas of low pressure, and you have a very complex picture (*see* diagram). Therefore, in northern latitudes air moving towards the pole is deflected to the right, forming the W and SW winds of temperate latitudes, whilst air from the arctic high is deflected to the left to give NE winds. Some of this moving air creates the winds that circulate the world at high altitudes, the jet stream, while the remaining cold air sinks at the poles and returns to the equator at the surface.

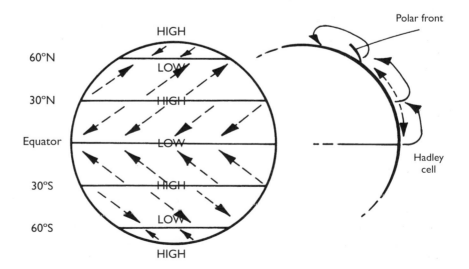

Pressure belts around the earth.

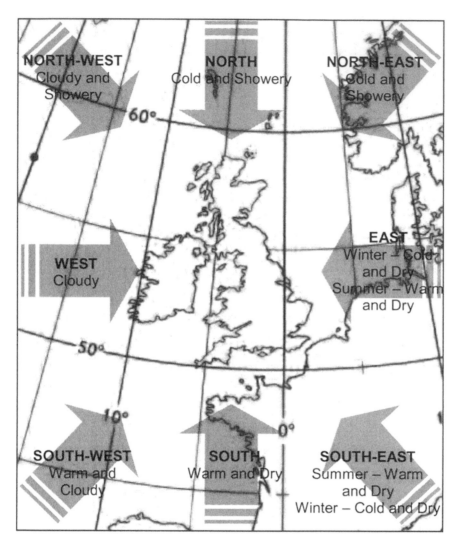

In northern hemispheres, where these cold and warm winds meet is known as the 'polar front'. The polar front is situated between 40 and 65 degrees of latitude but its exact position varies with the season, day to day and place to place. The UK is situated at the polar front and it is in this region that the fickle weather of temperate latitudes is created. The position of the polar front therefore determines whether the UK is in cold polar or warm tropical air. Due to the position of the UK, however, other factors influence and modify this flow and hence the weather. Air flowing over the Atlantic to the west adds moisture to the flow, whereas from the east the air is drier. A number of air masses have been identified that affect the UK.

What is the Temperature and Moisture Content of the Air Going to Be?

Think about where the air has come from, its moisture content and how cold the air is. As cold polar air moves southwards over an increasingly warm sea, the heating of the air by the sea causes cumulus clouds to form; these may grow enough for showers to develop. Warm air from the tropics is cooled from below. Sometimes the cooling is sufficient for fog to form or a thin layer of cloud that may produce drizzle.

When the air rises over coasts and hills the moisture comes out as clouds and if there is enough moisture then it can rain. This is why the west coast of the UK is generally wetter than the east coast. A moisture-laden air mass approaching the UK may still produce rain even if does not have any depressions and associated fronts. This is because as it rises over the land it expands due to the decrease in atmospheric pressure. This expansion requires energy, which is released from the cloud as heat, meaning the cloud cools. The result is that vapour condenses out, creating clouds and possibly rain if there is enough moisture or, if it is cold enough, snow. So we do not need depressions and fronts (*see* later) to cause poor weather, just moist air and heat.

In reality, the type of air mass affecting the UK only gives an indication of the weather that may occur. The actual weather depends on the history of the air, the speed of movement and the surface over which it flows.

Depressions and Anticyclones or Low Pressure and High Pressure

There is another more important way that the UK's fickle weather is formed. This is by the formation of depressions with their associated fronts. Airstreams have so far been described as being homogeneous masses, but it will not surprise many to realize that this is a much-idealized picture and the uneven warming of the land distorts the picture, making it more akin to a bowl of porridge with cold milk being slowly added.

A low-pressure system, also known as a depression, occurs when the weather is dominated by unstable conditions. Under a depression air is rising, forming an area of low pressure at the surface. This rising air cools and condenses and helps encourage cloud formation, so the weather is often cloudy and wet. In the northern hemisphere winds blow in an anticlockwise direction around a depression. Isobars are normally closely spaced around a depression, leading to strong winds. Depressions can be identified on weather charts as an area of closely spaced isobars, often in a roughly circular shape, where pressure is lower than surrounding areas. They are often accompanied by fronts.

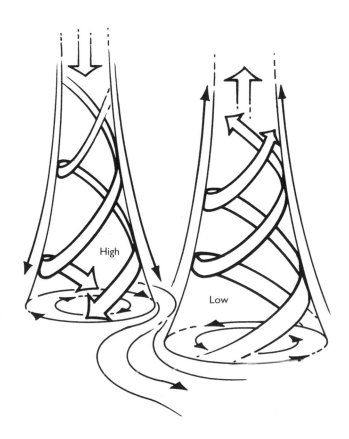

High and low pressure systems. A depression is an area of low pressure – the winds circulate in an anticlockwise direction. The converse of a depression is an anticyclone, which is an area of high pressure where winds circulate in a clockwise direction.

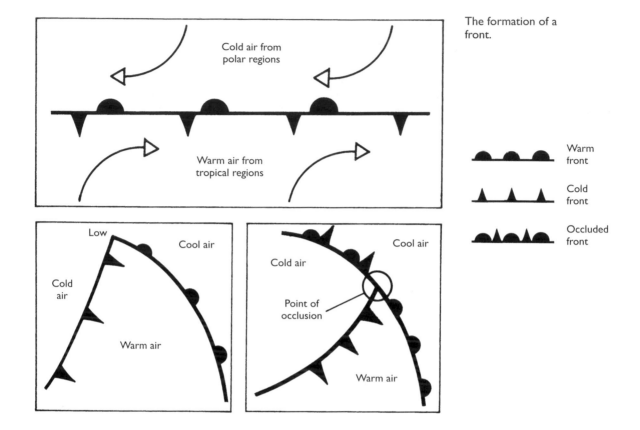

The formation of a front.

Warm front

Cold front

Occluded front

High-Pressure Systems

A high-pressure system, also known as an anti-cyclone, occurs when the weather is dominated by stable conditions. Under an anticyclone air is descending, forming an area of higher pressure at the surface. Because of these stable conditions, cloud formation is inhibited, so the weather is usually settled with only small amounts of cloud cover. In the northern hemisphere, winds blow in a clockwise direction around an anticyclone. As isobars are normally widely spaced around an anticyclone, winds are often quite light. Because the air is descending it inhibits the formation of clouds.

WINTER ANTICYCLONES

In winter the clear, settled conditions and light winds associated with anticyclones can lead to frost and fog. The clear skies allow heat to be lost from the surface of the earth by radiation, allowing temperatures to fall steadily overnight, leading to air or ground frosts. Light winds along with falling temperatures can encourage

fog to form; this can linger well into the following morning and be slow to clear. If high pressure becomes established over Northern Europe during winter, this can bring a spell of cold easterly winds to the UK.

SUMMER ANTICYCLONES

In summer the clear settled conditions associated with anticyclones can bring long sunny days and warm temperatures. The weather is normally dry, although occasionally very hot temperatures can trigger thunderstorms. An anticyclone situated over the UK or near-continent usually brings warm, fine weather.

Fronts

Air masses therefore have different properties, but what is more important for weather forecasting is what is happening where these air masses meet. The boundary between two different sorts of air is called a front. When cold polar maritime air meets warmer tropical maritime air, the warm air is forced to rise up over the colder air. In northern latitudes a front usually separates warm, moist air from the tropics and colder relatively dry air from the polar regions. As the warmer air rises and cools, water vapour condenses to form clouds and perhaps rain. The amount of rain associated with the clouds depends on the temperature contrast between warm and cold air. Fronts can vary from a thin line of clouds to heavy, persistent rain. The weather often associated with a depression is cloudy, wet and windy. The winds circulate in an anticlockwise direction. Let us look in more detail at the formation of a front. At a hypothetical front there is cold NW air to the north and warm SW air to the south. The barrier between the two air masses is moving and pressure differences between the cold and the warm air creates a distortion called a depression and with time this becomes distinct with warm and cold fronts developing. Because the cold front moves slightly faster than the warm

front it can catch up, lifting all the warm air above the colder air and forming an occluded front.

Fronts have typical cloud patterns associated with them that can extend several hundred kilometres ahead of the surface front and have a characteristic structure, which is easily recognized. Frontal systems tend to occur in 'families', which migrate in an easterly direction across the Atlantic. Sometimes as many as four or five mature depressions may make their way across the United Kingdom before a ridge of high pressure builds up to prevent any more from advancing over the country. The origin stage tends to occur over the mid-Atlantic, with the mature stage occurring over the United Kingdom.

Warm Front
Ahead of the depression in the cold sector, high cirrus clouds may occur in long feather-like streaks. Some cirrostratus may also occur up to

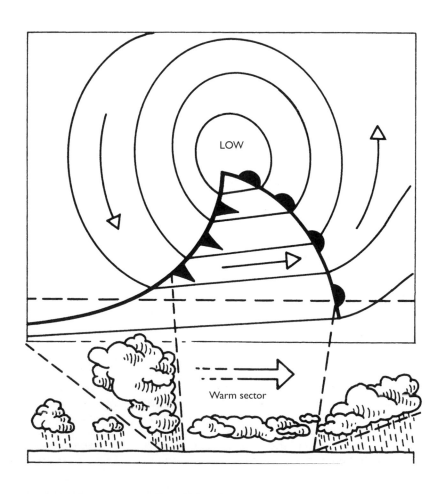

The method for showing a front on a weather map and what it represents on the ground.

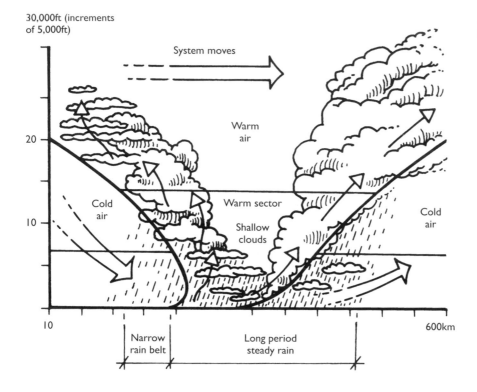

30,000ft (increments of 5,000ft)

A cross-section through a front.

System moves

Warm air

20

Cold air

Warm sector

Shallow clouds

Cold air

10

10

600km

Narrow rain belt

Long period steady rain

Clouds

Low clouds:

- cumulus – 365m (1,200 ft), cotton wool/cauliflower shaped, may produce showers;
- cumulonimbus – 30m (100ft), cumulous but reaches great heights, accompanied by heavy showers, perhaps with hail and thunder;
- stratus – 457m (1,500ft), grey, layered in ragged patches; if thin, the disc of the sun or moon will be visible (providing there are no other cloud layers above); if thick, it may produce drizzle or snow grains.

Medium clouds:

- altocumulus – 2,133m (7,000ft) or more, grey or white, several different types, the most common being either patches or a sheet of rounded elements, but may also appear as a layer without much form. Occasionally some rain or snow;
- altostratus – 2,438m (8,000ft) or more, greyish or bluish, a sheet of uniform appearance sometimes thin enough to reveal the sun or moon vaguely. May give generally light rain or snow.

High clouds:

- cirrus/cirrocumulus – 5,181–10,668m (17,000–35,000ft), composed of ice crystals, white, with delicate hair-like filaments, sometimes hooked at the end; sometimes its appearance in a regular pattern of 'waves' and small gaps may resemble the scales of a fish, thus giving rise to the popular name 'mackerel sky'.

960km (600 miles) ahead of the surface position of the warm front. As the front approaches, temperatures start to rise and barometric pressure falls steadily.

As the warm front passes over, drizzle and then rain will usually start to fall from altostratus

and nimbostratus clouds. The amount of cloud will increase and the cloud base will fall. Continuous rain will persist as pressure carries on falling.

In the warm sector, pressure stabilizes and the amount of cloud falls as the clouds start to thin out. The precipitation also stops, and the weather is generally fine, with a little stratus or stratocumulus. As the cold front approaches, pressures rise slightly and temperatures start to fall slightly.

Cold Front
As the cold front passes over, large, towering cumulonimbus clouds develop. This produces heavy downpours of rain and fierce squalls, sometimes with hail and thunder. Pressures rise steadily and air temperatures start to drop.

Behind the cold front there is an end to the heavy rain as the cumulonimbus clouds move away. Barometric pressure continues to rise in a steady fashion. A few showers may occur from some small cumulous clouds, but it is generally fine and cool behind the cold front.

The frontal system dies as the warm air has completely risen and cooled, and is now under-lain by the cold air. The differences in temperature have therefore been equalled out, and the occluded front disappears.

How Do We Judge the Severity of Weather?

It is difficult to tell how severe the weather is going to be just by watching the clouds. The strength and direction of the wind, air temperature and pressure changes will give us a much better indication. A slow drop in pressure means that the depression is long-lasting but not extreme; a sudden drop means the weather is going to be poor and last a shorter time. The pressure gradient relative to the pressure around the depression will dictate how severe the weather is going to be.

Here are a few points about movements of a depression:

- generally, the future movement of a depression is an extension of its previous track;
- depressions also tend to move from areas of increasing pressure to areas of decreasing pressure;
- the centre of the depression will move parallel to the isobars in the warm sector;
- depressions tend to move around large, stationary, high-pressure areas, i.e. anticyclones;
- a depression with an occluded front tends to move to the left of its track;
- high-pressure systems or anticyclones have no definite path of travel and may linger for several days before being pushed away by depressions.

Wind

Wind is the curse of sea kayakers. It generates the bulk of problems that arise, choppy seas, capsizes, wind chill, weather tide effects, surf and so on.

Paul Caffyn

Wind is created by air rushing from areas of high pressure to areas of low pressure along a 'pressure gradient'. These gradient or 'geostrophic' winds are then deflected by friction at the earth's surface. In the northern hemisphere, air is deflected to the right and the speed of these winds is directly related to the pressure differences.

The geostrophic winds should not be confused with the trade winds or jet streams at altitude. The high-altitude winds are responsible for the general direction the depression moves in, W to E. The geostrophic winds are those that we experience at ground level.

Winds associated with the depression rotate in an anticlockwise direction, parallel to the isobars, which on a weather map join up areas of equal pressure. The tighter these isobars, the steeper the pressure gradient and the stronger the wind. It can therefore be seen that if you sit in a kayak with your back to the wind, the centre of the depression is always to your left (Buys Ballot's law). Depressions or lows are sometimes referred to as cyclones. The wind is stronger in winter because the polar zone of cold air expands and the polar front shifts south.

An oft heard quote is: 'the Met Office got it wrong'. In fact a more accurate phrase would usually be: 'I interpreted the data incorrectly'. Force 4 is the normally accepted maximum wind strength for paddlers to operate in but this statement disguises a number of variables. The wind speed ranges from 11 to 16kt in a force 4. A 10kt wind produces a mean wave height of 0.4m, yet a mean wind speed of 20kt produces a mean wave height of 2m. By just moving outside the parameters of a force 4, the wave height has varied by a multiple of five and this could have serious consequences for inexperienced paddlers on the water.

Paddling into a head wind is also important. Burch in *Fundamentals of Kayak Navigation* states that a 10kt wind exerts a pressure of approximately 1 pound on the front of a paddler. Increase the wind speed to 14kt and the pressure doubles to 2 pounds. With 17kt of wind the pressure increases to 3 pounds. This wind resistance is roughly the water resistance that a paddler must overcome to make a kayak go 3kt in calm air. Basically, at 17kt you have to paddle twice as hard!

Coastal Microclimate

A microclimate is a distinct climate associated with a small-scale area. The coastal microclimate has land and sea breezes that are mild in winter and cold in summer. In the summer much of the coastline experiences sea breezes. The sun heats up the land, the warm air rises and cooler air is drawn from the sea to replace it. Sea breezes usually start during late morning and peak by mid-afternoon. They can reach force 3 or 4 and extend to 20nm off-shore. A tell-tale sign is a line of clouds along the coast. The opposite is seen during the evening as the land cools faster than the sea. The picture is not

---

Wind Speed and Direction

The direction given for the wind refers to the direction it comes from, e.g. a westerly wind is blowing west to east.

Wind strength is measured at 10m (33ft) above the ground. Wind speed is measured in knots. However, forecast winds are often given in mph (1kt is equivalent to 1.15mph). Wind speed is often given in terms of the Beaufort scale.

Gusts are rapid variations in wind speed and can be 60 per cent higher than the mean speed.

If you are in any doubt about the effect of wind upon you consider this:

- at 20mph it is 2lb/ft^2;
- at 60mph it is 12lb/ft^2.

If the wind force increases by three from 10 to 30mph, the force increases by nine.

---

as simple as onshore and off-shore wind – the prevailing wind must also be considered, as the coastal wind can increase or decrease the speed or change the direction slightly of the prevailing wind. Valleys can funnel wind and very steep cliffs can cause sudden down-draughts.

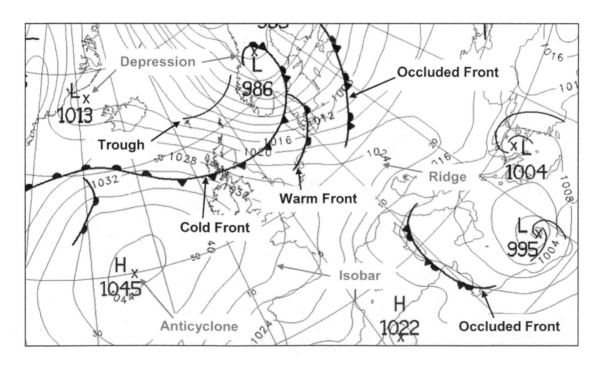

A weather chart. © Crown copyright 2006. Published by the Met. Office.

HOW TO READ A WEATHER CHART

Interpreting a weather chart looks difficult but it is really straightforward. A weather chart summarizes the movement of warm and cold air, high and low pressure, as well as the presence of clouds.

Principal lines on a weather chart are the isobars. These continuous lines or contours join up points of equal pressure in millibars, they identify features such as anticyclones (areas of high pressure), depressions (areas of low pressure), troughs and ridges, which are associated with particular kinds of weather.

High Pressure or Anticyclone

An anticyclone can be identified on a weather chart as a large area of widely spaced isobars, where pressure is higher than surrounding areas. In the northern hemisphere winds blow in a clockwise direction around high pressure. The highest pressure occurs at the centre. Anticyclones can bring warm and sunny weather in summer, but cold and foggy weather in winter.

Low Pressure or Depression

Often isobars form a distinctive thumb-print pattern, with low pressure at the centre; this is a depression or cyclone and is associated with strong winds and rain or snow in winter, depending on where the winds have been travelling from. Winds blow anticlockwise in low pressure areas and their strength is shown by the distance between the isobars: close together means strong winds; wider apart, light winds.

Troughs

Troughs are elongated extensions of areas of low pressure. They bring similar weather to that associated with depressions.

Ridges

Ridges are elongated extensions of areas of high pressure. They bring similar weather to that associated with anticyclones.

Col

This can be identified as an area of slack pressure between two anticyclones and two depressions.

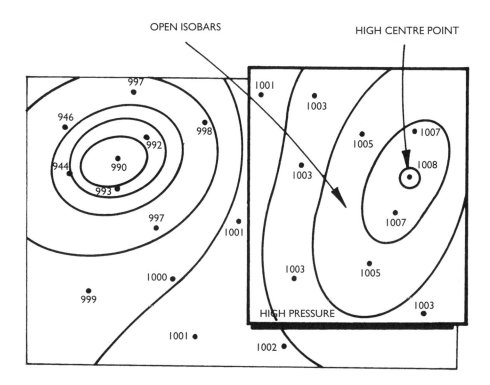

High-pressure systems.

Low pressure.

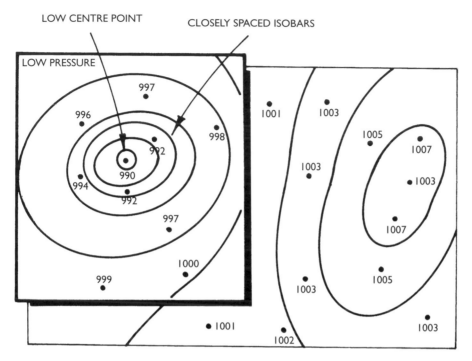

LOW CENTRE POINT   CLOSELY SPACED ISOBARS

LOW PRESSURE

997
996
998
992
990
994
992
997
1000
999
1001
1002

1001   1003
1005
1007
1003
1003
1007
1003
1005
1003

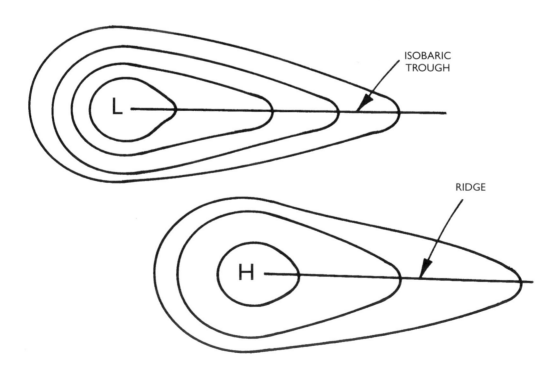

ISOBARIC TROUGH

L

RIDGE

H

A trough and a ridge.

A Col.

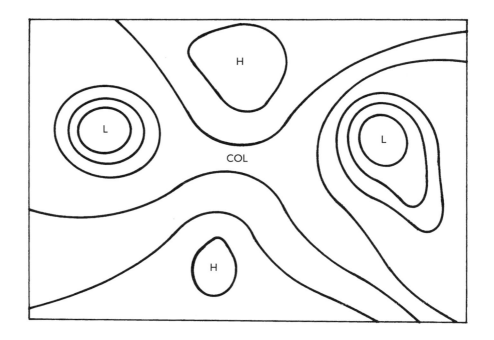

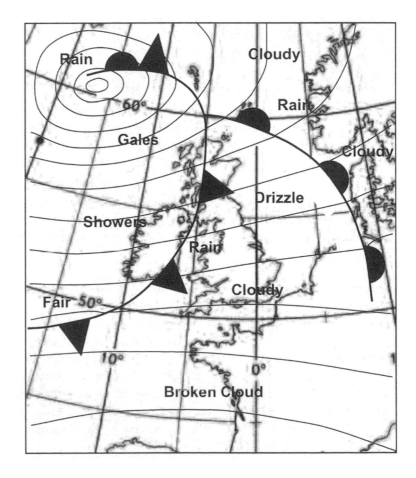

The weather patterns associated with a front. © Crown copyright 2006. Published by the Met. Office.

Weather Fronts

The side of the front that has the 'humps' or 'triangles' indicates the direction in which the front is moving. On a weather chart, the warm front is marked by a single line but this only marks its position on the earth's surface. The boundary between the air masses at the warm front is not vertical, it is a slope at a gradient of 1:150. In contrast, the slope on a cold front is 1:75.

Sometimes fronts do not bring much in the way of rain or cloud, and are then known as 'weak'. Thunderstorms can occur with all three types of front, but are most likely to accompany a cold front. However, many thunderstorms are not linked with frontal activity (*see* opposite).

Warm Front

Ahead of the warm front is a belt of thickening cloud, gradually developing into moderate rain and cloud. The belt of rain extends 160–320km (100–200 miles) ahead of the front. Behind the front the rain usually becomes lighter or ceases, but the weather often remains cloudy. The warm front does not necessarily bring higher temperatures. This is particularly so in summer, when the cloudy weather behind the front cuts off the heat from the sun. In winter, however, the south-westerly winds that usually blow after a warm front has moved through, bring milder conditions. The advance of a warm front is usually the way in which a cold winter spell is broken down. Ahead of a warm front pressure falls steadily, and sometimes very rapidly. After the passage of the front, the barometer usually steadies or falls less rapidly.

Cold Front

This usually brings a narrower belt of cloud and rain. It is called a cold front because the moist south-westerly winds ahead of it are replaced by cooler, drier north-westerly winds. When a cold front moves through an area it usually brings brighter, clearer weather behind it, but this brighter weather is sometimes mixed with showers. Pressure falls ahead of the cold front, but usually rises after its passage and the wind veers.

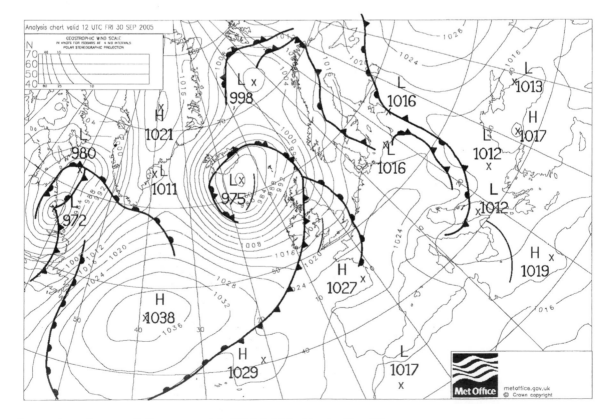

An actual weather map. © Crown copyright 2006. Published by the Met. Office.

Occluded Front or Occlusion

The characteristics of an occlusion are similar to those of a cold front in that the rain belt is narrow, and the winds generally veer to the north-west behind it. There is usually a clearance to the west after the front has moved through.

Thunderstorms

Thunderstorms are normally associated with cumulonimbus clouds (dark cumulus cloud). They are usually very tall and dark and form on warm sunny days as moist air near the earth's surface is warmed by the sun. As the air rises, it cools forming cumulus clouds.

Cumulonimbus clouds often have hail associated with them when rain drops are warmed and cooled as they rise and fall in the cloud.

Thunder and Lightning

Thunder is caused by extreme heating and expansion of air along the path of the lightning. Lightning is a large electrical spark caused by the movement of electrons in the cumulonimbus clouds; 90 per cent of lightening travels from cloud to cloud.

Lightning can also strike from great distances, up to 48km (30 miles) from its origin. One good

---

Humidity

Humidity is measured by looking at the difference between a wet bulb thermometer and a dry one. The heat of evaporation causes a drop in the temperature of the wet one. The drier the air, the greater the difference between the two. Exposed flesh works in the same way and results in the chill factor, e.g. with a temperature of 4°C and a wind speed of 15kt, the effective temperature is −3°C.

---

way to estimate the distance of a thunderstorm is to take into account the speed of sound. According to *World Book Encyclopedia*, the speed of sound in air is 335m/s (1,100ft/s), which means that it travels about a mile in five seconds. For example, if you see lightning and count to 15s, it is about 3 miles away.

Every person in Britain has a one in two million chance of being killed by lightning each year. This compares with a one in 8,000 chance of being killed in a traffic accident. Lightning kills an average of seventy-three people per year in the United States. This is more than the average number of deaths for hurricanes and tornadoes. A warning is buzzing of metallic equipment, and hair standing on end.

Several precautions can protect those out of doors during thunderstorms. Obviously, avoid

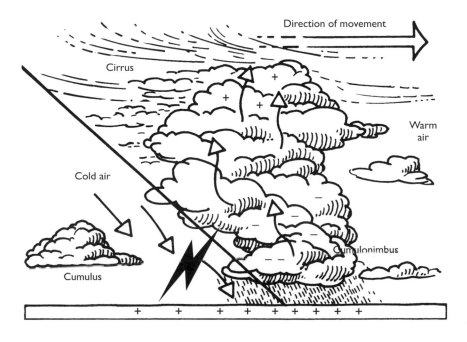

Thunder and lightning.

high exposed ridges with no cover. Avoid metals, such as aluminium paddles, as well as isolated trees. Seek cover in a low area that is heavily wooded with evenly sized trees. Stay low and keep your feet together.

Many lightning deaths are the result, not of a direct strike, but of a conductive injury that causes a cardiac arrest.

Hurricanes

A hurricane is a large rotating storm centred around an area of very low pressure, with strong winds blowing in excess of 72mph. The storm may be 10km (6 miles) high and 640km (400 miles) wide and it moves forward like an immense spinning top. They are formed when a warm sea heats the air and a current of warm air rapidly rises, creating an area of low pressure. This rising air is replaced by cool air around it and the rotation of the earth causes the rising column to twist. Hurricanes occur between July and October in the Atlantic, Eastern and Western Pacific north of the equator, and off Australia and in the Indian Ocean between November and March. Although the UK is not affected by hurricanes, we do get the remnants of hurricanes as large depressions. The most common phenomena associated with hurricanes are strong winds, very large waves up to 15m (49ft) high and rain.

Beaufort Wind Scale

One of the first scales to estimate wind speeds and the effects was created by Britain's Admiral Sir Francis Beaufort (1774–1857). He developed the scale in 1805 to help sailors estimate the winds via visual observations. The scale starts with 0 and goes to a force of 12. The Beaufort scale is still used today to estimate wind strengths. Wave heights quoted are approximately those that may be expected in the open sea. In enclosed waters, the waves will be smaller and steeper. Fetch, depth, swell, heavy rain and tide will also affect their height, and there will also usually be a time-lag between any increase in the wind and the consequent increase in the sea.

Force	Speed		Conditions
	kt	km/h	
0	<1	<1	Calm, sea like a mirror.
1	1–3	1–5	Light air, ripples only.
2	4–6	6–11	Light breeze, small wavelets (0.2m/8in). Crests have a glassy appearance.
3	7–10	12–19	Gentle breeze, large wavelets (0.6m/2ft), crests begin to break.
4	11–16	20–29	Moderate breeze, small waves (1m/3ft), some white horses.
5	17–21	30–39	Fresh breeze, moderate waves (1.8m/6ft), many white horses.
6	22–27	40–50	Strong breeze, large waves (3m/10ft), probably some spray.
7	28–33	51–61	Near gale, mounting sea (4m/13ft) with foam blown in streaks downwind.
8	34–40	62–74	Gale, moderately high waves (5.5m/18ft), crests break into spindrift.
9	41–47	76–87	Strong gale, high waves (7m/23ft), dense foam, visibility affected.
10	48–55	88–102	Storm, very high waves (9m/30ft), heavy sea roll, visibility impaired. Surface generally white.
11	56–63	103–118	Violent storm, exceptionally high waves (11m/36ft), visibility poor.
12	64+	119+	Hurricane, 14m (46ft) waves, air filled with foam and spray, visibility bad.

Fog

Visibility is another factor that needs to be considered when travelling at sea, especially when open crossings are going to be undertaken. The official definition of fog is a visibility of less than 1,000m (3,280ft). This limit is appropriate for aviators but for sea kayakers a limit of 200–500m (656–1,640ft) is more realistic. Early summer with its long hours of daylight and probable settled weather is an ideal time for sea fog ('advection' fog) to form on open water as a result of moist warm air being cooled over a cooler sea.

THE EFFECTS OF THE WIND ON THE SEA – THE CREATION OF WAVES

Everything from earthquakes to a ship's wake will create waves, but the most common cause is wind. The friction of the wind as it passes over the surface of the water creates ripples. It is a common misconception that the water is moving forward in a wave. In fact, the water itself does not move forward very rapidly – it is mainly travelling up and down in a circular, or rotary, motion. This is fortunate because if water was moving at the speed of most storm waves, it would make ocean navigation in ships nearly impossible.

How big a wave becomes will depend on three things:

1. The speed of the wind.
2. How long the wind blows.
3. The fetch.

Light winds, or those that only blow hard for a short time, cannot generate large waves. Storms of equal size generate much larger waves in the open Pacific than, for example, in the Adriatic Sea, where fetch is much more limited.

There are two different sorts of waves created by the wind: wind waves and swell waves.

Wind waves are produced by the prevailing local wind blowing over a long fetch of water. They move in the same direction as the wind – a northerly wind will produce southerly moving waves. They are generally confused waves.

Swell waves start off as wind waves in a storm out at sea, but the waves move away from the storm itself and continue across the ocean. Swell waves can come from any direction and there can be more than one set from different storms.

> **Wave Terminology**
>
> - Fetch is the distance of open water over which the wind is blowing.
> - Wavelength in metres, is the horizontal distance between successive crests or troughs.
> - Wave period in seconds, is the time between successive crests.
> - Wave height in metres, is the vertical distance between the top of a crest and the bottom of a trough.
> - Crest is the highest point on a wave.
> - Trough or valley between two waves, is the lowest point on a wave.

Groups of waves from storms in the Pacific near Antarctica have even been detected in Hawaii and Alaska, more than 10,000km (6,200 miles) away! They are often overlooked as a hazard but they should not be ignored, particularly when paddling on western coastlines where the prevailing weather comes from the northern hemisphere. Days with blue skies and flat seas can lead to a sense of false security because an unexpected swell running over rocks, a sand bar or into a sea cave at low tide can create breaking waves and can pose a serious threat, especially in times of poor visibility.

Swell waves are quite regular in length and height, but they do combine to form what surfers call 'sets'. Some waves cancel each other out, while others augment each other. This creates a regular pattern of small waves and large waves at the coast. To predict swell, look for storms on a weather map. In the UK a storm in the Atlantic will potentially create swell that reaches the coast 24–48h later. Look to see if any land will interrupt the swell and lessen its size.

Surf

In deep waters, only wave length and wave period affect a wave's speed. As the wave approaches shallow water, the ocean floor begins to affect the wave's shape and speed. Wave height increases, and the crests become more peaked. As the steepness increases, the wave becomes unstable. The forward speed of the crest becomes faster than the speed of the wave, and the wave breaks.

We can describe breaking waves in three different ways:

- Surging breakers – happen on beaches where the slope is very steep. The wave does not actually break, instead it rolls on to the steep beach. These kinds of breakers are known for their destructive nature.
- Plunging breakers – happen on beaches where the slope is moderately steep. This kind of wave normally curls over, forming a tunnel until the wave breaks. Expert surfers love this type of wave! Greatly increased by an off-shore wind.
- Spilling breakers – occur on beaches with gentle slopes. These waves break far from the shore, and the surf gently rolls over the front of the wave. Generally they occur with an onshore wind.

Beach Shape/Morphology

Wave size and shape are greatly affected by the profile and features of the beach, such as sand bars, rivers, rocks, piers and wrecks. Some of these features may only affect the surf at a certain height of tide because the profile of the beach changes as the tide falls or rises.

Dumping waves are steep and break very quickly and are usually very heavy! They are

> ### Wave Energy
>
> The energy of motion, in waves is tremendous. An average 1.2m (4ft), 10s wave striking a coast puts out more than 35,000 horsepower per mile of coast. If you doubt this, look at the damage it does when it hits the coast. For example, on the coast of Scotland a block of cemented stone weighing 1,350 tons was broken lose. Later, the replacement pier, weighing 2,600 tons, was carried away by waves. Off the coast of Oregon, the roof of a lighthouse 28m (91ft) above water was damaged by a 135 pound rock that was carried by the high waves.

caused by a very steep beach profile; on some beaches this may be only at the top or bottom of the beach.

When surf lands on a beach the water then has to find its way back out to sea. It does this by following natural channels on the beach, similar to stream beds. The water flows out towards this channel and then at 90 degrees to the beach; these currents are very strong and called rip currents. They can often be seen from the sea as they contain sand deposits and cause the surf to

Using a support stroke to 'Bongo ride' a wave.

Catching a wave.

be smaller or not to break. Undertows are caused when the water rushes back out to sea under the incoming surf. If caught in a rip, paddle/swim at 90 degrees to it or go with it back out to sea beyond the break-line where it will die out.

Other Sorts of Waves

Clapotis
Clapotis waves occur when an incoming wave meets a rebounding wave from a harbour wall, for example. The resulting crash sends the wave skywards.

Refracted Waves
When waves hit the coastline at an angle, the part of the wave closest to the land will slow down and bend round to reach the shore. This is called refraction and can cause waves to bend 180 degrees round headlands to hit sheltered shores. They can even create clapotis waves as they bend round an island to meet on the other side.

Wind Against Tide

When the tide and wind are going in opposite directions, the wind will hold the surface of the water back, creating or lifting waves up to make them larger. Combine a spring tide with an overfall and the wind against the flow, and some very violent seas can be produced.

Exposed and Difficult Landings

This is linked in part to swell and in part to the topography of the shoreline. Planning is the key element in this situation although at times it may be necessary to modify plans whilst afloat and force a landing in a more demanding area. The only way to prepare is to practise in controlled areas, but how often do we practise scrambling out of kayaks up cliffs. The attraction of the long sandy beach usually proves too strong for most people and surf landing and launching is something which must be practised, first in small waves and then increasing sizes.

Tidal Races

Most paddlers have heard horror stories of tidal races around the British Isles, but most of them can be avoided by prior planning. Passing at or near slack water is the correct solution if there is any doubt but it is important to remember that slack water does not necessarily occur at high or low tide. When passing through it is often possible to sneak through on the inside close to the coast rather than in the middle where the water is flowing at its fastest. At many locations it is possible to land and inspect the tide race in the same way one would do a rapid on a river. This approach is a good option if leading a group in unknown waters.

When the tidal race flows over a sea-bed constriction, such as a sand bar or headland poking out into the sea, it can create a very turbulent sea called an overfall, where the waves are bigger and more varied than predicted by the wind speed. As the tide drops and the underwater obstruction comes closer to the surface, the water can become even rougher.

Other Hazards at Sea

Shipping and Other Water Users
The last few years has seen the introduction of large high-speed ships operating in the Irish Sea and on some cross-channel routes. They are a major hazard to kayaks and should be avoided at all costs. They have a blind spot of about half a mile, a distance that takes less than a minute to cover at the speed they travel! Most of the time they are relying on radar to pick up other water vessels and they are not expecting to see kayaks. The only advice is to find out their schedules and paddle at another time or in a different area.

In comparison to these vessels most other craft are fairly harmless – although the boy racers on their evening trips back from off-shore parties are a hazard at night. It is all very well knowing the rules of the road but remember 'might is right' – a bow wave at close quarters is not an experience to repeat!

Marine Wildlife
There are number of animal species that can prove hazardous to paddlers, especially if paddling in more distant waters. There is always the temptation to paddle closer to inspect any thing that is seen but this is not always to be recommended. Off Race Rocks, Vancouver Island, an irate sea lion chased a paddler who had inadvertently disturbed it whilst feeding. It dropped its catch and went after the paddler. Various species of shark bumped Paul Caffyn

Beware of other boats – they cannot always see small kayaks.

whilst he paddled around Australia, and in warm waters there is always the risk of sea snakes.

Cold water creates its own problems. Those paddlers fortunate enough to spend time in the Arctic have to pay attention to polar bears and even in lower latitudes it is necessary to adopt bear etiquette. Encounters with bears can be relatively common off the west coast of America.

Many paddlers dream of meeting whales but there are occurrences of paddlers being capsized by whales off Baja. This may be the result of getting too close to the young or it may just be an accident. If a collision occurs, it is not hard to imagine who comes off second-best in the encounter.

On a smaller scale, many paddlers enjoy the prospect of shellfish at the end of the day, but often care needs to be exercised when collecting them. Anybody who has experienced food poisoning as a result of eating contaminated shellfish will testify that it is not an experience to savour. If it were to occur on off-shore islands it could prove a major problem, at the very least ruining several days of precious holiday.

Fishing vessel.

CHAPTER 6

USING THE KAYAK

PREPARATION FOR PADDLING

This should consist of three phases: warming up, increasing range of movements (ROM), and mimicking the movements of kayaking. Stretching has little benefit at this stage and is best kept for the end of a paddling session.

Warming-Up

Before anyone jumps out of their vehicle and leaps into a kayak they should ask themselves whether their body is prepared for the stresses about to be placed on it by kayaking. Even a very simple warm-up, such as jogging on the spot, will reduce the likelihood of injury. The aim of a warm-up is to increase the blood supply to the muscles, bringing oxygenated blood and nutrients, and removing the waste products built up while sleeping and sitting. Raise the heart rate gradually and increase muscle temperature slowly. The duration and range of a warm-up should increase in relation to the environment about to be entered – flat water requires less than surf.

OPPOSITE, ABOVE AND OVERLEAF: Warming up before paddling.

Warming up before paddling *(concluded)*.

The safety box. The term safety box is an imaginary box that extends as far as the hands when the arms are extended downwards to the top of the shoulder and in line with the body.

Range of Movements (ROM)

Joints are only lubricated when they are moving, therefore slowly and gently take each joint through their range of movements to lubricate them. Only move them in the directions they normally work in.

Mimic Kayaking

Finally, make the sort of movements you are likely to make when kayaking, this will help to wake up the brain/muscle link.

Lifting and Carrying

Following a warm-up, adopt some simple methods to lift and carry equipment – your back is very vulnerable, so protect it:

- share the load with heavy equipment;
- keep the range of movement within the safety box;
- keep your spine in line, bend the knees and look up when lifting;
- where possible, slide and glide the load, e.g. use a trolley.

Share the load when lifting and carrying a kayak.

PADDLING STROKES AND TECHNIQUES

Efficient paddling will depend on how comfortable and snug the paddler is in the kayak; this will ensure that all the effort put into making the body move is transferred to the kayak. A good fit is ultimately a balance between a tight fit and a fit that enables the paddler to relax when at sea for extended periods. To achieve a comfortable yet snug position, take the time to choose the correct equipment that feels comfortable and reduces the chance of injury, for example use the correct paddle length and degree of feather, adjust the back rests, footrests and hip pads.

The Importance of the Body/Boat Link

The most important piece of equipment is the paddler themself, because this is the engine that drives the kayak, the rudder that steers it and the brain that plans and executes any movement of it. Therefore, whenever a new technique or skill is learned, address the body first, then the kayak and finally the blade (body, boat, blade). This is because it is the body that moves the paddle or edges the kayak. The blade is simply an anchor for the body to rotate against, thereby moving the kayak in its desired direction. For this reason strokes and manoeuvres are described primarily from the body perspective.

Sea kayak keyhole cockpits – effective boat control depends on a well-fitting cockpit.

Propulsion

Forwards Paddling

The most important facet of forwards paddling is to have a range of gears that will enable the paddler to cope with the changing environment of the sea. The technique used or rate of forwards paddling will be different when cruising on a sunny day, paddling against the wind or punching out through a surf break. Even experienced paddlers can improve their forwards paddling technique to prevent injury and get more miles to the chocolate bar. There is no single way of forward paddling but there are some things to consider.

There are three phases to forward paddling:

- The catch or plant. It is important to plant the paddle as far forward as possible with a clean, stabbing entry. This sets up the blade for the next important phase of the stroke. Sit upright and avoid excessive forward body lean.
- The pull. With a craft in excess of 4.5m (18ft), its ability to go in a straight line (directional stability) is going to be relatively high. All your effort must therefore be used to drive the kayak forwards. Keep the blade vertical in the water and as close to the kayak

---

Use Your Head

All the strokes will be more effective if you look where you want to go. If you look down that's where you will probably end up!

How Many Gears Do You Have?

Practice the coaching points described in this chapter and note the changes in your technique, speed or endurance.

The catch.

The plant.

The phases of forward paddling.

The exit.

as is practical, much the same as an old paddle steamer.

- The exit. Pull the blade out when it reaches level with your hip, lifting your hand towards your ear, slicing the blade out of the water. Try not to lift the water – it will only push the rear of the kayak downwards.

Coaching points for forward paddling:

- Raise the top hand: this will encourage a more vertical paddle shaft.
- Rotate your trunk: allow the top hand to slightly cross over the centre line of the kayak,

thereby allowing the larger muscles of your shoulders and back to be used. This will allow you to paddle further/longer than by using just your arms.

- Look where you want to go, not at the paddle. Keep your head still – do not bob it up and down.
- Pull the kayak past the paddle. Use the top hand to extend and guide the paddle forwards. Extend the fingers of the top hand

---

Paddle Grip

Generally the paddle is held shoulder-width apart with equal distance between the hands and blades. By marking this distance with tape, the paddler can see when their grip varies.

Visualization Exercise

Imagine a large vertical sheet of paper on your right-hand side whilst you are sitting in the kayak. In your right hand is a marker pen, nib towards the paper. Paddle forwards and scribe a shape. What shape is it? It should look like a rectangle. The most common problem is that paddlers tend to round off the corners. Practise until the corners are nearly right angles.

to reduce the desire to push, this will prevent injury and cramp and give greater reach.

- Generally, paddlers push with their feet on the same side as they are pulling the paddle. Try putting your knees together to encourage a cycling action with the legs, spreading the load to all parts of your body.
- Sit upright – most paddlers tend to lean back slightly, so bear this in mind and think about your position from time to time.
- Keep the paddle shaft away from your body.

Hand Position During Forward Paddling

At first paddlers tend to keep the top hand low because it feels more stable. As they improve, stability comes from pulling on the paddle and, therefore, the optimum is attained – maximum forward propulsion with increased stability.

- Immerse the blade fully, vertically and at 90 degrees to the kayak.

Reverse paddling – good trunk rotation is essential.

Reverse Paddling

This is a very useful stroke for manoeuvring in caves, surf and slowing down or stopping the kayak. Here are some coaching points to think about when reverse paddling:

- look where you are going;
- keep your body upright to prevent the rear of the boat dipping into the water;
- push the blade forwards.

Trimming and Edging the Kayak

Trimming the kayak is the fore and aft change and edging is the side to side change. Trimming and edging the kayak are important because they will affect the whole performance of the kayak in many strokes.

> **Kayaking is Like Driving a Car**
>
> When driving a car, is it easier to steer sitting very close to the wheel or at bent arms length away from the wheel?
>
> - Try steering with a relaxed grip.
> - Look where you are going, not at the steering wheel!

Trim is generally altered by leaning forward or backwards or distributing kit fore or aft in the kayak. Once initial wobbles are overcome, edging is controlled by the lower body, whilst the upper body remains perpendicular to the water. As the paddler edges the kayak and

Edging – look down and you see the spray deck.

Leaning – look down and you see water!

Edging a kayak shortens the waterline length.

looks downwards, they will see the spray deck, if they lean and look down they will see water and if they are not travelling fast enough usually end up in it! (Much the same as a cyclist going around a bend.) Some coaches call this 'below decks paddling'. It is a technique that, once mastered, will increase your paddling potential and also reduce the likelihood of a capsize. To edge to the left, lift the right knee or tense the right leg, relax the left leg and push down with your left buttock and lean forward slightly. Apply the opposite for edging to the right, but remember to relax the right leg and keep your head up over the centre line of the kayak and, finally, look where you are going!

A low brace.

Terminology

Paddlers often use brace support and recovery to describe one stroke. However, the stroke can actually be divided into two. The dictionary definition states:

- a brace is a device that clamps and supports things in position, e.g. low brace turn, bracing into a wave;
- recover means 'to regain to a normal state or position', e.g. low or high recovery strokes.

Support and Recovery Strokes: Low and High Braces

These techniques help to stabilize the kayak and will be very useful in preventing a capsize when caught by a wave or a gust of wind. Before introducing the paddle into these strokes it is important that edging the kayak and righting it is mastered. Use external support if necessary, such as the side of a swimming pool or the front of another kayak. When the stroke is used to recover the kayak from tipping over, the knee lift and hip rotation must be timed to correspond with the blade hitting the water. Technically the execution of all support strokes is the same, although the side of the blade used may differ.

Low Brace Support
Coaching points for the low brace support on the right-hand side (do the opposite for the left-hand side):

- look where you want to go;
- lift your right knee, relax your left foot and push down with your left buttock and lean forward slightly;
- keep your elbows up, the shaft horizontal and push down on the back of the right blade;
- to recover the blade, roll your wrist forward so that the leading edge of the blade comes out of the water;
- stay within the safety box.

High Brace Support and Recovery
The high brace is executed in much the same way as the low brace except that the elbows are kept low and the hands high. The paddler then pulls down on the drive face of the blade. Remember to keep within the 'safety box' and keep the paddle in front of your head.

Moving Sideways: the Draw Stroke

Draw strokes are useful to position the kayak side-on to another kayak in a rescue or when approaching a rock or quay side to get out.

Simple Draw Stroke
Coaching points for the draw stroke:

- look where you want to go;
- keep shoulders parallel to kayak;
- hold the paddle shaft so that your hands are above each other;
- take the bottom blade and place it roughly 60cm (2ft) from the kayak;
- pull the paddle towards your hip;
- slice the blade out of the water and towards the back of the kayak;
- keep your hands in the normal paddling position;
- think safety box – if the top wrist has a watch on it you should be able to read the time;
- keep the knees neutral, i.e. no edge or, in deep-keeled kayaks, edge towards the paddle slightly;
- repeat.

ALTERNATIVE METHOD
Once this has been mastered, try the following: go through the first five coaching points for the draw stroke, then twist your wrist (control hand closest to the water) so that the blade slices back through the water at 90 degrees to the kayak. The kayak should travel parallel through the water. If this is not happening, try pulling the blade towards the front or the back of the kayak.

Top Tip

When trying to improve your stroke, try to gauge, score or measure your strokes on a scale of 0 to 6. Number the extremes as 0 and 6 and put yourself somewhere on the scale, e.g. scoring for trunk rotation when forwards paddling.

- 0 = no trunk rotation, you are just paddling with your arms.
- 6 = your elbows are locked; you could even tape them up and paddle, remembering to keep the blade close to the boat;
- now paddle with your normal style.

To help, you could get someone to time the runs or better, get them to video you.

Draw stroke – look where you are going.

Sculling Draw

The sculling draw enables the paddler to move the kayak sideways for a longer period because the paddle remains in the water and is constantly gaining purchase on the water.

Coaching points for the sculling draw:

- look where you want to go;
- keep shoulders parallel to kayak;
- hold the shaft so that one of your hands is above the other;
- the hand closest to the water controls the shaft;
- slice the blade forwards at approximately 45 degrees;

- slice the blade backwards at the same angle;
- each time the blade is sliced, the paddler resists the paddle moving away from the kayak and gains purchase to move the kayak sideways;
- the action is repeated linking into a fluid sculling action.

Top Tip: Close Your Eyes

When practising complex strokes like the sculling draw, close your eyes. This will help you to feel the stroke better and to concentrate on muscle movements.

Turning Strokes

Many sea kayaks can be fitted with a rudder that is effective in helping the kayak go in a straight line and in turning it – when they work properly, that is! The following explains how to turn the kayak effectively without the aid of a rudder. Learning these first, means that the rudder can be used, at a later date, with greater effect. Turning can be divided into small and large alterations of course.

Small Alterations of Course
The majority of the time in a kayak is spent travelling forwards, so the following strokes and techniques will help the paddler to make small alterations to avoid obstacles or keep on course.

EDGING/TILT TURNS
When the kayak is paddled forwards and edged at the same time, the underwater profile of the kayak changes from symmetrical to asymmetrical (creating a high-pressure side and a low-pressure side in much the same way as an aeroplane wing); this encourages the kayak to turn. In 90 per cent of designs the kayak will turn away from the edge or towards the knee that is lifted, i.e. lifting the right knee to engage the left edge will turn the kayak to the right. Edge away from the blade – this allows for greater leverage and also creates a better flow of water under the keel of the kayak.

THE KEY-HOLE STROKE
The key-hole stroke allows the paddler to power forward and steer in the same stroke. It is a combination of a forward power stroke followed by lowering the top hand and drawing the blade to the back of the kayak.

STERN RUDDER
When using stern and bow rudder or low brace turns, the kayak must be moving forwards for

Tilt-turning a sea kayak.

Using a stern rudder – keep your hands low.

them to be effective; they are therefore described as dynamic strokes. The longitudinal stability and momentum of the sea kayak makes the stern rudder very useful for small alterations of course. It is especially useful when paddling in a following sea (waves coming from behind the kayak).

Coaching points to think about when using the stern rudder:

- allow the blade to trail to the stern of the kayak, vertical and with the power side closest to the hull;
- keep your hands low;
- keep the shoulders parallel to the kayak;
- look where you want to go;

- hold the shaft away from the body;
- push away and pull with the stern hand;
- stay within your safety box;
- if you need more space, lift out the blade and replace it further from the kayak;
- with greater forward momentum, e.g. surfing, the blade can just be twisted by rolling the control hand closest to the water.

BOW RUDDER

In its purest form the bow rudder, when used in a sea kayak as opposed to a general purpose kayak, puts a great strain on the upper body. Nevertheless, in its varying forms it is still a very useful stroke for making small alterations of course, especially in confined spaces.

The sequence of using a bow rudder.

Coaching points for the bow rudder:

- paddle forwards gently;
- initiate the turn with a sweep stroke on the opposite side of the kayak to where you want to turn;
- place the paddle in the water (close to where your feet are positioned) in a draw stroke position;
- open your control hand slowly;
- move the blade forwards;
- look where you want to go to;
- increase turning by opening the hand further or moving the blade further towards the bow of the kayak;
- to blend or link the stroke, pull the blade into the kayak and then into a forwards power stroke. By moving the blade back, the kayak will eventually move sideways parallel to its existing course – this is commonly known as a hanging draw.

CROSS-DECK BOW RUDDER

The cross-deck bow rudder can be more comfortable and enable the paddler to edge to the outside of the turn, thereby reducing the drag from the keel. Try this stroke as you become comfortable with bow rudders and are able to mobilize your upper body.

Coaching points to think about when practising the cross-deck bow rudder (for a turn to the left):

- paddle forwards gently;
- initiate the turn with a sweep stroke on the right-hand side of the kayak;
- take your right blade over the front of the kayak and place it in the water (near your feet) in a draw-stroke position;
- open your control hand slowly;
- move the blade forwards;
- look where you want to go to;
- lift your left knee and edge to the right.

HANGING DRAW

In real terms a hanging draw is a bow rudder performed beside the kayaker with the paddle blade placed so that the kayak moves sideways parallel to the original course.

Coaching points for the hanging draw:

- paddle forwards gently;
- finish the forward stroke on the side that you wish to draw to;
- slice the blade forwards and open the hand, therefore increasing the blade angle – the kayak should move sideways;
- the draw can be adjusted by moving the blade forwards or backwards;
- take care not to slow the kayak down by opening the blade too much.

Larger Alterations of Course

HAND-BRAKE TURNS

This is really an advanced form of edging. By edging the kayak to a greater extent we begin to use the rocker on the edge of the kayak to decrease the waterline length of the kayak, thus reducing drag. Once mastered, the tilt or edge turn can be used to an extent where it is possible to turn the kayak in its own length. To increase the effect of edging on turning it is possible to combine it with sweep strokes.

A hanging draw.

A cross-deck bow rudder.

SWEEP STROKES

The sweep stroke is an excellent stroke for turning in tight spaces. It is greatly improved by using a combination of both forwards and reverse sweeps combined with optimum edge. If the most efficient forwards paddling technique requires the blade to be close to the kayak, then using the blade as far away from the kayak as possible will optimize turning.

Coaching points for the forward sweep:

- keep the top hand low;
- look in the direction you want to go;
- place the paddle in at the toe and out at the hip;
- stay within the safety box;
- edge towards the blade, this allows for greater leverage and also creates a better flow of water under the keel of the kayak.

Coaching points for the reverse sweep:

- keep the top hand low;

> ### The Difference Between a Sweep Stroke and a Draw Stroke
>
> A sweep stroke is when the blade is taken away from the boat, while a draw stroke is when the blade is taken towards the boat.

- look in the direction you want to go;
- place the paddle in at the back of the kayak and out at the hip;
- stay within the safety box.

SWEEP AND SCULL

These two strokes encourage a greater degree of edge and therefore a more efficient turn.

Coaching points for the sweep and skull:

- keep the top hand low;
- look in the direction you want to go;
- place the paddle in at the toe and out at the hip;

A sweep stroke – keep the top hand low.

- stay within the safety box;
- edge towards the blade, this allows for greater leverage and also creates a better flow of water under the keel of the kayak;
- return the blade to the front of the kayak in a low brace position – the blade should only 'kiss' the water; this way speed is maintained and the blade is ready for a low recovery stroke if necessary;
- repeat;
- remember to keep the kayak on edge throughout the turn.

Extended Paddle

The Inuit taught us, through the design of their paddle, the importance of using the whole length of the paddle. It is very useful sometimes to have a greater lever to turn the boat.

Practise moving your hands up and down the shaft to increase/decrease the lever. In an emergency try putting one hand on the blade.

Top Tip

Practise strokes on both sides – if you only practise on one side, you will never be a true master of the kayak.

LOW BRACE TURN

This technique gives the paddler a feeling of security and makes it possible to edge the kayak further therefore improving its turning circle. It is usually used when turning in tidal races, where the power of the water supplies the turning force.

Coaching points for the low-brace turn to the left:

- paddle forwards then initiate the turn with a sweep stroke on the right side of the kayak;
- look where you want to go to;
- lift your right knee to engage the left edge of the kayak;

An extended paddle.

- apply a low brace on the left side, allow the blade to skip over the surface of the water to prevent it acting as a brake;
- lean forwards.

Handling Wind and Waves

A Beam or Quartering Wind
A beam or quartering wind is when the wind blows at 90 or 45 degrees to the kayak. This is probably the sea kayaker's nemesis because most sea kayaks, like a windvane, will try to turn into the wind. There are several ways to counteract this:

- Use a skeg. Contrary to popular belief, the skeg has more than two positions, up and down. Try adjusting the skeg's position to give optimum benefit.
- Trim. Loading the stern of the kayak or dragging a towline on the stern can reduce the tendency for the wind to blow the stern of the kayak around.

A low brace turn.

- Increase windage on the bow of the kayak to stop the stern wandering by making the bow lighter, so it sticks up in to the wind more, or place a helmet on the front deck.
- Edge into the wind – this will encourage the kayak to turn away from the wind.
- Move your hands along the shaft towards the blade furthest from the wind. This has the effect of pushing the paddle out further on the windward side by increasing the lever.
- Aim for a point further upwind. Allow for the wind (leeway) on a crossing by pointing the kayak away from where you are going.

Waves

Paddling in waves is the true skill of a sea paddler and once perfected it is a joy to 'become at one with the waves'. What this really means is, relax and use the waves to help rather than hinder progress. This is best highlighted when paddling in a following sea. If executed proficiently, the paddler can use following waves to cover a good distance with minimum effort:

- paddle gently, with the waves;
- look where you want to go;
- as the back of the kayak rises, increase your paddle rate, the kayak accelerates and surfs down the wave;
- use a stern rudder to steer, combined with forwards paddling to maintain speed;
- when the kayak's speed reduces, slow the paddle rate and await the next wave (only increase paddle rate when going downhill!);
- use the peaks of the waves to turn on, as the ends of the kayak will be clear of the water. It may take several crests to turn the kayak the required amount. Try experimenting with sweep strokes and edge to make the optimum turn.

Rock Hopping

Rock hopping through rock 'gardens' is one of the greatest tests of your technical ability, but it needs to be combined with a bit of thought! Helmets are a good idea. Timing a rock hop is essential; because waves come in sets, some join to grow bigger, some cancel themselves out. Generally the first of the set is smaller than the last and then it starts again. Watch the waves and then time your run. Useful strokes when rock hopping are the stern rudder, hanging draw and low support.

LAUNCHING AND LANDING THROUGH SURF
Launching

When the sea is big it can often seem that there is no way of getting off the beach. Sometimes this is actually the case and it is often better to wait either for the tide to change, or to move down the coast. However, as we become more experienced at watching the sea it is possible to look at the beach and work out a way through, in much the same way as a river paddler looks for a line down a river. If you do find yourself being surfed backwards, the kayak will naturally turn parallel to the wave. Lean forward and use a low/high support stroke on top of the wave to stay upright. Paddle forwards or backwards to avoid obstacles, or a draw stroke to slow you down. If at any time you think you might hit another water user, capsize to slow the kayak.

Problems to look for include:

- Any obvious hazards, e.g. rocks, rip currents or other water users.
- Rip currents: these are good for getting out back (behind the breakers) as the water is moving that way and is often calmer. It is important to be aware of the consequences of a swim in a rip. The force of the water means that it is pointless to swim towards the beach, even though that is the natural response. Remain calm and swim parallel to the beach, the rip will soon dissipate enabling the swimmer to turn and use the energy of the waves to progress towards the beach.
- Wave sets: remember waves work in sets, time them and try paddling out just after the largest waves of the set. Wait just before the break-line and time your paddle out.
- Look for natural breaks in the waves and zig-zag your way out back.
- PLF – paddle like fury – approach the waves in an aggressive and positive fashion. Remember the forward paddling tips: dynamic forwards paddling, vertical paddle shaft close to kayak, trunk rotation, forward trim.
- Plant the blade and pull to anchor (stop it going backwards) the kayak as you go through the wave. If a large wave rears up ahead of the kayak and it is inevitable that it is going to break on you, then it is important to increase power. Lean forward so that your face does not have to absorb the full impact. When the wave hits, place the blade deep in

Launching the kayak through surf.

the wave, trying to gain purchase on the more solid deeper water as opposed to the aerated upper layers, and attempt to pull yourself and the kayak through into the calmer water beyond. It is important to keep the paddle fairly low across the body as the wave hits. If it is held too high, there is the possibility that the force of the wave could drive the shaft backwards and into the teeth of the unsuspecting paddler.

- Be prepared! If it is obvious that you are going to fail to break through the breaking wave, then be prepared to slip readily into the brace position.

In most situations it is preferable if one paddler is designated to leave the beach last, in order to help steady kayaks, help with spray decks, retrieve paddles that have been washed away and, finally, to ease the kayak over the sand and rocks, thereby preserving the hull of the sea kayak. This is especially important if the launch involves weaving through rocks. This extra assistance is generally appreciated by the other paddlers. If the boulders are large or awkwardly positioned and the waves are rolling in, then the last person to launch may be better off swimming out, especially if he/she is prepared for immersion in the water.

Ideally the kayak should be just floating as the paddler steps in. If the water is calm, then it is preferable to have the kayak parallel to the beach, although in many instances this is not possible. With a relatively large cockpit it is possible to just sit down and then slide the legs underneath the deck. With smaller cockpits it may be necessary to sit on the rear deck of the kayak and then slide the legs in at the same time as lowering oneself onto the seat. It may be necessary to scull with the paddle at the same time as lowering oneself onto the seat. Although this may sound a difficult and unstable exercise, it is relatively easy to accomplish after a small amount of training and it certainly helps to avoid damage to the kayak.

As a general rule, launching stern first is the favoured option. Essentially this is because skegs, modified hulls and rudders, are in deeper water sooner and therefore less liable to damage from contact with rocks and other underwater obstructions.

In all difficult launches the priority has to be to protect the kayak and the paddler from damage. Sometimes when landings have taken place on off-shore reefs or where there is a steep section of coastline, as the tide rises and falls the situation can vary significantly. An option, if the water drops deep quickly, is to throw the kayak in to the water and jump in afterwards. If there is any chance of the kayak being blown away then it is advisable to attach yourself to the craft. If there is a swell surging up the rocks, the desirable time to launch the kayak is as the wave surges to its peak. If the kayak is launched at that moment, as the wave sucks back, the kayak will be taken away from the rocks and the area of potential damage.

Landing

On steep beaches, dumping waves are likely to be encountered and this can be a potentially dangerous situation because of the amount of energy that is released when the waves break. When landing, the trick is to be in control, which is not always the case when surfing on the front of the wave, therefore stay on the back of the wave whenever possible. In extreme cases, if you have to land and injury is a major concern, consider swimming in and pushing the kayak in front of you. The following gives greater control when landing, especially on unknown or dumping beaches:

- Assess the landing: choose the best spot. Look for hazards, e.g. onshore/off-shore wind, dumping waves, obstacles, rips, people in the water, lifeguard zones, flags. If the dumping waves are in a relatively small bay, one way of identifying the easiest landing place is to watch the seabirds, if any are present. They will tend to sit on the water in the area of least disturbance. If there are birds on the water do not just paddle blindly in, it is still important to monitor a number of waves, but if there are gulls on the water it highlights an area that is worthy of particular attention.
- Allow the waves to pass under the kayak, reverse paddle if necessary. Once the breakline is reached allow the wave to pass under the kayak, then try to remain behind or on top of the wave.
- Get out quickly and drag your kayak up the beach – release the spray deck beforehand to aid a fast exit.
- Be prepared to help the others – the first person to land should not just stand there admiring the scenery or laughing! Their

Paddling sea kayaks in a tidal race can be exciting.

responsibility is to grab the front of the arriving kayaks and either gently pull them until they ground or at least hold them so that the paddler getting out does not slip and receive an unwelcome swim at the end of the paddle.

Paddling in a Tidal Race

In Chapter 3, the formation of tidal races was examined; how they are affected by wind speed and direction and whether there are spring or neap tides. Sea kayakers will inevitably come across tide races that act very much like large

rivers, therefore it is appropriate to use the same terminology associated with manoeuvring in tidal races as for river paddling.

- Paddle with the flow: be alert and watch for turbulence in the water.
- Paddle against the flow: either paddle hard or use available eddies (where the flow of water is opposite to the main flow caused by rocks jutting out or isolated rocks in the water).
- Ferry glide: taken from the time when ferries use to cross rivers at an angle rather than straight across. Lift the upstream knee to

The features of a tidal race.

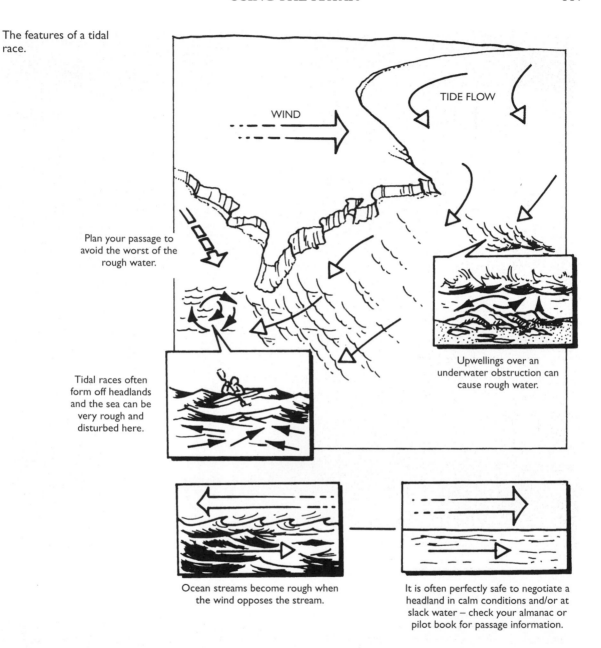

WIND

TIDE FLOW

Plan your passage to avoid the worst of the rough water.

Tidal races often form off headlands and the sea can be very rough and disturbed here.

Upwellings over an underwater obstruction can cause rough water.

Ocean streams become rough when the wind opposes the stream.

It is often perfectly safe to negotiate a headland in calm conditions and/or at slack water – check your almanac or pilot book for passage information.

edge the kayak downstream and paddle confidently across the current, minimizing the distance it would drift downstream. Speed is crucial to punch through the confused water between the eddy and the main current (the eddy line).

- Breaking in: this is used when you need to get from the eddy back into the main current. Paddle with commitment across the eddy line at an angle of 110 or 130 degrees. Lift your upstream knee and edge the kayak downstream. Adopt the low brace position, look downstream. Relax once the kayak is parallel to the main current.

- Breaking out: when you need to get from the main current into an eddy, paddle towards the eddy and, with commitment, across the eddy line. Lift your upstream knee and edge the kayak downstream. Adopt the low brace position, look downstream.

Capsize drill.

1. The paddler is upside down, exhale – this helps to keep calm.
2. Bang on the bottom of the kayak to signal others.
3. If able, stay in the kayak and move your hands, palm outwards forwards and backwards along the gunwale. This will set up the kayaker for an Eskimo rescue.
4. To exit the kayak, pull the spray deck release strap, knees together, head forward and push with the hands.
5. Keep hold of the upturned kayak and paddle if possible, and await rescue.

If the flow is less powerful, the turns can be initiated with sweep or power strokes when breaking in and out. Once mastered, the joys of paddling and surfing tide races can be truly appreciated.

RESCUES

The sea is an unpredictable beast. Expect the unexpected and endeavour to gain every piece of knowledge, not every piece of rescue kit. Sea paddling would lose some of its excitement if everything always went to plan, so be prepared for the worst. With all incidents at sea, the emphasis should always be on self-sufficiency and not reliance on external aid. However, there are times when speed is of the essence and outside emergency help must be sought, for example a heart attack. All sea paddlers should be able to summon help and co-ordinate the rescue. However, never lull yourself into a false sense of security by thinking 'It's OK if anything happens, a helicopter is just around the corner', it may be rescuing someone else!

With all rescues the priorities are not to endanger yourself unnecessarily and to look after the casualty first and the kayak second. This includes not injuring yourself, especially your back by unnecessary lifting – a laden sea kayak is extremely heavy.

Protect Your Body When Rescuing Another Paddler

The UK Health and Safety Commission guideline weights for lifting are 25kg reduced to 15kg with arms extended, which is further reduced by 20 per cent when twisting to 90 degrees. It goes without saying that a swamped laden sea kayak far exceeds this.

Ultimately, when we need to, we have to lift, but there are a few steps we can take to reduce the strain on the body:

- Most sea kayaks are fitted with a bulkhead just behind the seat. By lifting the bow of the kayak, the water will drain away. When the bow is not obvious, use paint or stickers to aid identity. When the bulkhead is large, inflate an airbag behind the seat to lessen the amount of water that can collect there.
- If the situation is not serious and the swimmer competent, use them to assist you.
- Use other paddlers to assist when it is safe to do so.

Prevention Is Better Than Cure

1. Know your limitations.
2. Plan your paddling with knowledge of tides and weather.
3. Dress appropriately and carry emergency kit.
4. Check equipment works and is in good repair.
5. Practise rescues to ensure they are quick and efficient.
6. Tell someone where you are going and your return time.

T-rescue or X-Rescue

This is the most common form of rescue to return a swimmer to their kayak:

- communicate clearly: tell the swimmer to keep calm, hold onto their kayak and swim, if possible;
- instruct the swimmer to hold onto the bow (front) of the rescuer's kayak.

When the swimmer is in a dangerous situation, for example close to rocks, there are two options depending on the situation. The paddler's judgement will determine which one to execute.

- If it is necessary to remove the swimmer quickly from imminent danger, the swimmer should hold onto the rescuer's bow whilst the rescuer paddles to safe water or land, leaving their kayak behind.
- As above, but the rescuer clips their towline to the swimmer's kayak and paddles to safe water.

The T-rescue can now be executed.

1. Grab the bow of the upturned kayak (the bow can be recognized by the footrest bolts or by added markings), if extra support is required, lean onto the upturned kayak.
2. Place the bow of the kayak on the cockpit and hip flick up. In most case this is enough to break the water seal. Twisting the kayak also achieves this. Allow the water to drain, the remainder can be pumped out later.
3. When it is calm enough, the swimmer can assist the rescuer by either sinking the back of the kayak or pulling the bow from the other side.

Using a stirrup to aid the rescue of a swimmer.

The scoop method.

Getting back in, between
the sea kayaks.

OPPOSITE AND ABOVE: Both T- or X-rescue methods.

4. Right the upturned kayak and place the paddles across the cockpits to stabilize the raft.
5. Get the swimmer back into their kayak.

'Eskimo' Rescue/Bow Rescue

Tips Before Using the Eskimo Rescue
Before attempting the Eskimo rescue, the

What to Do With the Paddles During a Rescue

If the swimmer is competent, then they can hold the paddles. If not, the rescuer can store them either under their decklines or in a paddle park/leash (a short length of line and clip attached to the kayak or paddler, that can be wrapped around the paddle shafts).

---

following building blocks should be put in place:

● practise edging: using the bow of a partner's kayak, practise righting the kayak – remember to keep the nose of the rescuer's kayak within the safety box, i.e. in front of your head;
● practise on both sides and progress from maintaining a grip on the nose of the kayak to the kayak coming in from a distance.

If a paddler is confident to stay in their kayak following a capsize, the 'Eskimo' rescue is quicker and avoids total immersion of the upturned paddler. The capsized paddler simply hangs in their seat with their arms raised, banging on the hull for attention. Arms are swept backwards and forwards hoping to find the bow of the rescue kayak, upon which the victim hoists themselves out of the water.

A rafted X-rescue. When it is not possible to rescue the swimmer's kayak, a third paddler can raft up with the rescuer to assist.

Tips for the Rescuer
The standard bow presentation Eskimo rescue:

- approach at 45 degrees in front or behind the paddler's hands – this avoids injuring the paddler and gives the victim more chance of grabbing the resuer's kayak;
- keep forward momentum as the paddler rights themselves, this will avoid the rescued paddler pushing the other kayak away.

An adaptation of this method, useful when paddlers are parallel with each other and the upturned paddler's hands have been missed the first time:

- instead of presenting the bow of the kayak, the rescuer lays their paddle shaft across the upturned kayak and their cockpit;
- the rescuer takes the paddler's hand and places it on the paddle shaft;
- the paddler rights their kayak – the rescuer needs to allow a gap between the two kayaks to enable this.

Rescuing an unconscious paddler.

Towing

Towing is a means by which a paddler can transport an incapacitated paddler and kayak to a safe location.

Contact Tow

Possibly the easiest method. The paddler requiring a tow grabs on to the rescuer's kayak either at the bow or stern, forming a raft. The rescuer simply pushes or pulls them to safety. For a quick release the rescuer can simply shout 'let go'.

Towlines

For tows over a longer distance a towline is required. The towline can be one of the paddler's most useful and versatile piece of equipment, but it does have its limitations. Consider making or adapting a towline in order to design a system that is efficient and adaptable in all situations.

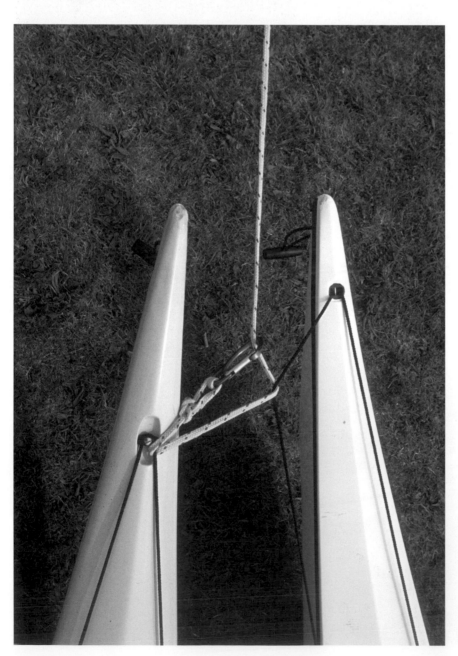

Clipping on to a boat.

Towing.

Before purchasing a towline consider the following:

- How easy is it to use and repack, especially with cold fingers?
- Is the gate on the clip large enough to clip onto a kayak's fittings and strong enough to cope with the stresses?
- Fast deployment is essential in situations where the victim is close to rocks or drifting rapidly – check how fast it can be deployed.
- Does it have an integral shock absorber and a quick release mechanism?
- Is it long enough?
- Does it float?

Where to Attach the Towline
OPTION 1
For comfort, the optimum anchor is on the kayak, usually by means of a fairlead (eye) and a jamming cleat fixed on the deck behind the cockpit. When fixing the eye and cleat, make sure a strong backing plate and large washers are used to spread the load. Having the tow in the middle of the kayak allows for greater manoeuvrability (a harbour tug has the anchor dead centre).

OPTION 2
The second, more common, option is towing via a waistbelt. This has the advantage that it travels with the paddler and can be transferred to another paddler to use.

Length of Tow
Most towlines carried by sea paddlers are too short, but there is no definitive answer to the best length. Initially a towline of approximately 1.5 kayak lengths is recommended for the following reasons:

- it allows a raft of kayaks to be clipped together (essential to avoid kayaks pulling apart and reducing stability);
- it prevents the towed kayak from bumping into the back of the towing kayak.

Daisy-chaining a towline. A daisy-chained towline is an easy way of shortening and lengthening a tow line. It also makes it possible to clip in anywhere to reduce the length further.

The length of line should be flexible and it should be possible to extend the line either with another line or, where the system allows, for example daisy chaining, releasing more line. In a following sea, the towline must also be long enough to prevent the towed kayak from surfing into the back of the towing kayak.

Throwlines
Many paddlers carry a throwline to throw to a swimmer when the situation is too serious for the rescuer to go in and paddle with them, such as in caves and gullies. They are probably the easiest method of carrying extra line.

An in-line tow.

Sharing the Tow

If the distance to be towed is large, consider sharing the tow by swapping over the towline or by adding more kayaks, either in line with the original towing kayak or in a fan tow, where rescuers attach to the deck lines of the kayak in front of the cockpit.

Rafted Tow

In some instances the paddler being towed may be incapacitated, which is likely to make them unstable in their kayak and need reassurance. Support can be provided by rafting them up with another paddler to create a stable platform. When towing two kayaks, always pass the towline through both sets of decklines.

Anchored Rescue

The anchored rescue allows a T-rescue to be executed without fear of being smashed on to the rocks, blown downwind or disappearing downtide. It is also an excellent method for manoeuvring a raft to use as a platform for administering first aid or repairing equipment.

- Whilst one paddler begins to rescue the swimmer and kayak, another attaches their towline to the end of the rescuer's kayak.
- The paddler who is towing, now tows away from the danger, upwind, away from rocks, into the waves, uptide or towards the nearest eddy, thus anchoring the rescue.

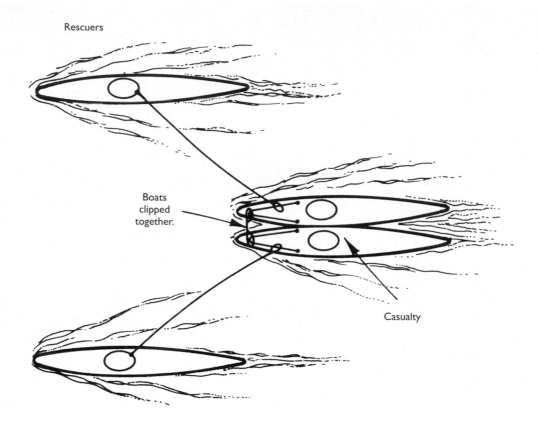

Rescuers

Boats
clipped
together.

Casualty

A fan tow.

- If a third paddler is unavailable, then to avoid being blown downwind, it may be possible to clip your helmet or sea anchor to your towline. This can be dragged in the water and will act as a drogue and slow down the rate of drift.

Rescuing a Double Sea Kayak

Double sea kayaks can be rescued in much the same way as singles. However, when fully laden and in a rough sea, it is more effective to right the kayak, empty one cockpit and, whilst one paddler paddles, the other pumps out. Modifications on this are for one person to get in whilst their crew balances the kayak and this is then repeated for the crew. Paddle floats have their benefits to assist the balancing of the kayak.

Rescues in Surf

Surf is too chaotic and potentially hazardous to attempt T-rescues or to use towlines. The rescuer's role is to escort the swimmer to safety, with the swimmer holding onto the seaward end of their kayak (whether that be front or back) and kicking their legs to push themselves towards the beach. If the swimmer becomes tired they can either hold on to the rescuer's kayak and be towed in or, if possible, get on to the back of the kayak in a piggyback/pillion position. If caught in a rip current, encourage the swimmer to swim parallel to the beach away from the rip.

The Eskimo Roll

For early Inuit/Eskimo hunters, swimming in freezing water was not an option; they therefore perfected methods for rescuing themselves

An anchored rescue.

A rescue in the surf – get the kayak later!

The sequence of getting back into a double sea kayak.

whilst remaining in their kayaks. Exit was also made near impossible due to the fact that their Cag or Tuvilik was actually sewn on to the kayak. The simplest and most effective system of self-rescue is to perfect the 'Eskimo' roll – this is the pinnacle of many paddlers' abilities. However, this can often put an inexperienced paddler under enormous self-imposed pressure, which is often a factor when rolling fails. Imagine the Inuit hunter sewn into his kayak if he is alone on the water and capsizes, then he has only one choice to roll – that is real pressure! Once acquired this skill will boost the paddler's confidence immeasurably and is well worth the persistence to practise until perfect.

There are many types of roll but here we will describe the basic 'screw roll'. The reason for using this roll is that the paddler maintains the normal paddling grip. When perfected on both sides it allows the paddler to right themselves in most conditions. Any roll must be practised in the appropriate craft, because rolling a fully laden sea kayak is very different to rolling a small general purpose boat at the pool.

Underwater Confidence

When upside down in a kayak, the first thing to address is confidence. Try the following to improve your confidence:

Exercises for Confidence

Remember to wear a hat or plugs to prevent water entering the ear, which can lead to surfer's ear.

- capsize, exit the kayak and place your head into the air pocket formed by the cockpit;
- with a partner, repeat the exercise and swap boats underwater;
- once upside-down relax, close your eyes, blow bubbles through your nose, or/and hum a song;
- practise your hip flick – this is the vital part of the roll, practise and practise on both sides.

The Blade

During a roll, we are aiming to do a combination of a sweep and high recovery stroke ... only upside-down! The following will help you to have a greater understanding of what is required:

- capsize without the paddle, reach up with both hands on the same side of the kayak;
- a partner, standing in the water, can hold the paddle at the side of the kayak in the 'set up' position;
- grip the paddle in the normal paddling position;

OPPOSITE AND ABOVE: The partner guiding the paddle helps when learning to roll.

The sequence of rolling a sea kayak.

The sequence of rolling a double sea kayak.

- the standing partner can now guide the paddle through the roll manoeuvre;
- practise until the movement is understood;
- now practise setting up from a variety of paddle positions;
- practise wearing full kit;
- now try it in rougher water.

Common mistakes:

- rushing – roll when are ready;
- head coming up first – keep your head low with your ear on your shoulder;
- paddle diving – feel for the surface of the water with the blade before commencing, alter your wrist angle, keep dry elbow bent and low;

- too much grunt and not enough technique – use smaller blades or relax your grip on the shaft;
- capsizing at the end of a roll: either start your hip flick earlier or at the end of the roll return the blade to the front of the kayak in a reverse sweep or low/high recovery position.

Some difficulties encountered when rolling a sea kayak:

- in calm water the boat tends to lie on its side preventing the paddler from rolling up on a favoured side – practise on both sides!;
- in windy conditions, a larger kayak will catch the wind more, making it easier to roll up into the wind;

A paddle float. An inflatable pocket that slips over one blade whilst the other blade is held under the deck lines and acts like an outrigger.

A search-and-rescue
helicopter.

• in tide races, the paddler's body will be
carried downtide of the kayak, making a roll
on this side much easier.

Solo Re-Entry

There are many methods of solo rescue dependent on the kayak and the competence of
paddlers. With practice it is even possible for
one or both paddlers in a double sea kayak to
re-enter and roll. This is not a common
manoeuvre when paddling with groups, but it
may be a useful technique to have up one's
sleeve. The two most common methods are to
re-enter and roll or to use a paddle float to stabilize the kayak whilst you get back in. Both
should be practised in rough water as this is
where you are most likely to need it.

Re-Entry and Roll

- Lay the kayak on its side, with the paddler's preferred rolling side towards the wind and waves.
- Grip the cockpit rim firmly and cradle the paddle in the arm on the preferred side.
- Take a deep breath and tuck your legs into the kayak.
- As the kayak settles upside-down, set up for the roll.
- Only when settled, attempt to roll – an extended paddle stroke can be used to boost confidence.
- The hard part is to paddle to a position where the spray deck can be put on and the kayak pumped out. A paddle float can be used to stabilize the kayak.

Paddle Float Re-Entry

Using a paddle float can increase stability hugely. The inflatable float bag is pulled over one blade and can be used to either roll or as an outrigger at the side of the kayak. This enables the paddler to climb on to the deck with ease, even in rough conditions. Carrying a paddle float may seem to be over the top but it does work and is extra security for a paddler who does not have a bomb-proof roll.

External Rescue

Methods for attracting attention were examined earlier. Let us now assume that help is at hand either from a lifeboat or helicopter. From the outset it is important to remember that the crews of these vessels are highly skilled. If in any doubt about what to do, do nothing until told what to do by the crew. The best place for a casualty to be picked up from is either the water or the front or back of a raft of kayakers. To prevent the raft from blowing away, it can be towed by another paddler.

When dealing with a helicopter rescue there are some important hazards to be aware of:

- Downdraught: helicopters create a powerful downwind strong enough to capsize a paddler and blow away equipment. Ensure that the group are rafted up or paddle hard into the draught and brace. Stow kit in hatches or tie it down.
- Noise: helicopters are very noisy, which can be both alarming and deafening. Brief the group well before the helicopter is overhead.
- Static: this is an electrical charge built up by the helicopter as it flies through the air. It is discharged when the winchman or wire touches the sea or the paddler! It may be wise to to turn off GPSs and radios.

CHAPTER 7

LEADING AND EXPEDITIONING

TO LEAD OR NOT TO LEAD?

Experience is not what happens to you.
Experience is what you do with what happens to you.

Aldous Huxley

The leader is normally the person in the group who has the most experience and has the ability to ensure that a group works together well. Whenever we are in the charge, or care, of other people whom we trust are good at their job, our safety may depend on it. Whenever the going gets tough, we depend on their skills, experience and expertise to deal with it calmly and efficiently. If you are the one leading, you will be expected to be good at your job.

Somebody once paddled half-way around Ireland against the tide because they could not read a pilot book. This is an extreme case, which fortunately did not have an unpleasant ending, but there must be a large number of similar incidents. It is therefore up to you to ensure that you have the technical competence, knowledge and understanding, so that the trust that the group has in you is not misplaced. The more that is known about a particular topic the better, it not only increases safety but it usually enhances enjoyment of the day:

● for the leader because they can relax;
● for the group because they learn more.

A leader must develop technical competence to such a level that it is automatic and be able to focus on the group whatever is happening. Learning to lead trips is a similar evolutionary process to learning to kayak.

To lead a group of paddlers on a day or weekend trip can be a great thrill, as the group have put their faith in your skills and expertise. With this faith, however, comes responsibility. Being a leader is not about being paid or having a contract – we all have a legal 'duty of care' to

those around us every day. In the context of a group of sea paddlers (two or more), the standard of care owed to the group is higher for the more experienced member, which may or may not be the leader. If an accident occurs, the most experienced member may be asked to explain what they did or why they did not intervene to prevent the accident. If you are not willing to accept responsibility, do not put yourself in a situation where you will be deemed to be responsible.

SAFETY AND RISK REDUCTION IS AN AWARENESS OF DANGER

Accidents are not usually caused by a single incident. Imagine a trip where the wind picks up and the temperature drops, neither of which is an immediate threat. However, combine them with a paddler who has forgotten lunch, drink and warmer clothing, and the cold paddler now slows down. The paddler becomes tired and the tide turns. With wind now against the tide, the waves grow in size. The cold paddler becomes increasingly tired and cold, slowing down even more as they battle with the elements. If the paddler had brought pogues, a bobble hat, food and drink, they would not have a problem. If the leader had thought about wind against tide before the trip, they may have planned a different trip. Nevertheless, we are all human

---

Duty of Care

The duty that rests upon an individual or organization to ensure that all reasonable steps are taken to ensure the safety of any person involved in any activity for which that individual or organization is responsible.

Leading a group
of sea kayakers.

and as a result are fallible; we leave late, transport breaks down, we spend too long in a bay or on an island, or we simply overestimate our abilities.

Making decisions is an integral part of sea paddling. Route choices, equipment, paddling partners, food selection – on and on goes the list of decisions we make before, during and after our adventures on the water. Many paddlers make seemingly spontaneous decisions, relying on past experiences, training and gut instinct to guide them. For the most part, the consequences of these decisions are minor; after all, who really cares if we have pasta instead of rice for dinner? In other circumstances, decisions do

have a direct impact on our personal safety and the safety of the people with whom we paddle. For example, the decision to paddle an injured friend across a large bay at night to get to medical help is a serious one, affecting the safety not only of the injured paddler, but the rest of the group as well.

Safe sea paddling should be seen as an awareness of danger, not a series of rules and regulations. Following a set of rules and regulations, thinking that disaster can be avoided, is tempting fate. Unfortunately, good judgement only comes with experience and the ability to listen to the messages the environment is giving us. It cannot be taught easily since it cannot be written down with hard, fast rules. No rules or technology can ever replace the need to watch for changes in the sea and the wind. While there are always factors beyond our control, like the weather unexpectedly changing, we can cut down on the risks dramatically by common-sense actions, such as checking the weather forecast and tide tables, being aware of local hazards, always wearing a PFD, having the required safety gear, taking some lessons and paddling with a partner.

An important role as a leader of sea kayaking trips is that you can keep risk at an acceptable level. But what is acceptable? Acceptable risk is not easily defined and is dependent on a variety of social and personal factors. Perceptions of risk also differ, for example a parent may perceive sea kayaking as dangerous and horse riding safe, whereas from your viewpoint the opposite may well be true.

We should also remember, as leaders, that the conditions we find challenging may frighten the living daylights out of our group. A leader cannot rely on the group members to react competently in situations where they are under stress; therefore be careful when putting yourself in a position where safety depends totally on the group members' actions and reactions.

Part of managing risk is that leaders put aside their personal ambitions; their desire to kayak is secondary to the needs, desires and safety of the group. However, it is also important that the personal ambitions of the group are secondary to safety. For some people, the drive to achieve a goal can lead to unnecessary risks being taken. The desire to achieve the goal may be linked to a number of things. It might be because of a commitment to a sponsor, it might be the result of a long-term wish or it might be as a result of the need to get back to the mainland in order to get to work on time. Whatever the cause, unfettered ambition can compromise safety and should be treated with caution. The skill of an experienced leader in being safe is doing the right thing at the right time, that is, having judgement. This may seem a simple concept but it often takes courage and experience to do it well, for example 'bailing out' of a situation and having to justify why the group did not complete the trip. The process of learning to be safe involves the transition from recreational paddler to leader and depends on training and experience but most importantly self-analysis. Where were we at greatest risk? Could we have done

something different? Risk is frequently thought of in terms of physical injury but we should also consider the psychological effects of what we do.

Safe leadership is a matter of judgement, what worked well in a given place at a given time may not be appropriate in the same place at a different time. Judging the situation by protocol or rules invites disaster. Leading in a safe manner means considering the consequences of everything we do, asking the question, 'What if' and learning from our experiences. Ultimately safety and risk reduction is about being aware of danger – but remember, what is dangerous for one group may not be dangerous for another. Rules and regulations will only limit the experiences an experienced leader can provide for a group.

Like all aspects of sea kayaking, leadership can be made less stressful by sound preparation and planning. Remember, when you are a leader, it is hopefully because you have the most experience and skills. If you get in trouble who is going to help you? Play it safe.

Every sea paddler whether a leader or not should get into the habit of assessing risk. It is essential for outdoor centres, schools and the like, to have written safety policies but even club leaders should assess the risk, remember the leader is usually the most experienced paddler and therefore responsible if an accident occurs. You may be asked questions about whether you had identified the hazards, calculated the risk and either tried to reduce the risk or omit it. Most of the hazards are the same every time you go on the sea, but the group's ability to cope with the hazard will depend on many factors. A good leader will be assessing the risk dynamically and asking the question 'what if' all the time, for example what if my group all capsize here, if the answer is nothing but wet people you are fine but if your answer is more serious you need to do something about it! Below are some questions to ask yourself if you are leading.

On Land

- Do you know the area, including likely hazards as well as exit points. Basic information can be gained from coastal maps and sea charts. Always identify possible landing sites before starting out – sites that could be used if things do not go as planned. It is nearly impossible to have a detailed look at a map in big seas.

- Do the group have the paddling ability to complete the trip safely? It is best to determine this well before the trip, as it can be difficult to tell someone they cannot do the trip after a 0500 start and four hours of driving. If in any doubt about new paddlers' abilities, ask them to do an easier trip first to see how they perform.

- A group size of four to ten people is manageable. If there are more than this number of paddlers, then split them into small groups with each group having a leader and back-person.

- Details of the trip and expected finish time should be left with someone responsible who can notify the authorities if serious problems are encountered. This could be a partner or friend. Do not forget to contact them as soon as you return safely. Spending an unplanned night on a beach (or river) is a common occurrence and part of the adventure of paddling in remote areas, so this should be no cause for alarm. Callout time should be left with the responsible home person, but as a guide callout times are a day for overnight trips and four hours for day-trips.

- If you have a portable marine radio, then a further precaution can be to notify the coast-guard. However, do not rely on them, as only limited details can be left and reception is not guaranteed.

- Do you and the group have the right clothing for safety? This is especially important for beginners. Buoyancy aid, correct fitting spray deck, helmet or hat, secure footwear and appropriate clothing (thermal underwear, woollens, spray jacket, wetsuit) to stay warm in all anticipated conditions, or the reverse for hot days (sun hat and cream, spare water and so on). Less experienced paddlers will often get colder than more experienced paddlers because they are likely to timidly wait around while others play and explore, plus they tend to swim more often. Spare dry clothing should also be carried to increase warmth or if a walk out is necessary. Beaches become very cold and windy places when you have to wait for a car shuffle.

- Do you and the group have personal safety gear? Boats should be up to scratch with deck lines front and rear, grab loops and positive buoyancy (bulkheads and waterproof hatches and/or foam or airbags), and each member should have a whistle. Should any delays be encountered, spare clothing, basic shelter such as a large plastic bag or reflective foil blanket, and food make waiting more enjoyable.

Do You Have Group Safety Equipment?

- Do you have a weather forecast? In nearly every accident, a change in weather had a part to play.

- Have you briefed the paddlers before getting on the water? What the group should expect on the trip, what you expect from them and what procedures you require them to acknowledge throughout the trip. This is the most important part of trip planning. As the leader, you have done all the planning and know of problems you are likely to encounter – but no-one else in the group will know unless you communicate it to them. Also, identify where the safety gear is and nominate the front and last person.

On the Water

- Some people may need more time to adjust to the conditions and may approach a tossing sea with a degree of trepidation. It is important to allow people to paddle at their own pace, ensuring they are not pushed into paddling conditions that are more than they can handle. It can be hard to encourage faster paddlers to remain with the group and sometimes it is not necessary when the sea is calm but it needs to be explained to 'speed demons' that, if the paddle is advertised as a beginners trip, then everyone should be paddling at beginners pace and not at racing pace. Another way is to pair up a 'speed demon' with a beginner and get them to teach basic skills to them.

- The positioning of the leader and any assistant will depend on the trip, the sea state and the abilities of the group. Position yourself where you will be of most use – the position of 'maximum usefulness'. Put yourself between the group and danger, downtide, downwind, between the group and rocks. You may nominate a back person but keep an eye out for him/her. With novices the leader is normally in the lead and the back person is the second-best paddler. Any other good paddlers can be spread throughout the group.

Buddy up. When conditions become bad, reduce the distance between paddlers to maintain contact. If the distance reduces to a state where there is a possibility of collision, then it is about time to think 'Should we be here?'

- Before running a tidal race, entering a cave or landing in surf, for example, take time to examine the sea and what is happening. When are the sets coming through? When the group is running a difficult or dangerous gauntlet or beach landing/exit, the leader should direct proceedings; this includes directing experienced paddlers to safe 'catching' positions, whether it is on the beach waiting to catch boats and swimmers, or if it is a good paddler who is waiting in the lee of rocks so that he/she can help if things go wrong.
- If a rescue is necessary, the leader directs it using other members of the group rather than getting involved, unless speed is of essence.
- A good leader knows when to turn back. If sea conditions become such that it can no longer be paddled safely due to wind swell or chop, the party should take the quickest and safest method out of there, including finding somewhere to land quickly, then either walk out or camp the night.
- The leader also has the responsibility to direct someone to land and walk out (or turn back) if it becomes clear that they will be unable to complete the trip in safety. This is one of the hardest things you will have to do as a leader, but remember, the safety of the group is only as strong as its weakest link. Of course, it is better to ascertain someone's skill level well before they get on the water.
- The leader sets the example and helps with moving gear and boats.
- The leader communicates with the group.

PRACTISE MAKING DECISIONS

Scenarios to Work On

Like all decisions there are many correct answers and many wrong answers!

1. Six paddlers are out for the day. Four of the group are beginners and the other two are of good intermediate ability. The group is well-equipped and all boats have adequate flotation. Early in the day the group rounds a headland and suddenly encounters choppy, confused seas. One of the beginners tips over and bails out. He loses contact with his boat and paddle. Both begin to blow away. How should the trip leader keep the group safe while rescuing the victim? Split the group and take beginners to shore? Stay together?

2. You are with a group of four other paddlers out on the NW coast of Vancouver Island. Everyone in the group is an intermediate. You are planning to paddle 11km (7 miles) south. It has been drizzling and overcast for three days, but the weather is beginning to break. You put in at 0930. By 1100, the sun is out and the wind is up to 15kt. You are paddling in big swells that seem to grow bigger by the minute. You cross a reef area and suddenly all around you are huge boomers. You are very concerned that a wave may break over you. You are not sure how to get to shore because the surf is up and it looks treacherous. What are you going to do, short of paddling to Japan?

3. You and two friends are on a Sunday paddle in Pembrokeshire from Whitesands round Ramsey Island. It is late October. One friend dumps and bails out. He cannot roll and conditions are calm enough, so you try a rescue. His boat has a fair amount of water in it. You haul it up over the boat and while emptying it out, a paddle breaks. He then tries to haul himself into his boat but cannot manage it. He is getting tired and cold. He decides to try a paddle float rescue because that is what he is used to. Using the paddle float, your friend successfully hauls himself onto his own deck, but in the process of turning and wriggling down into the boat, his right leg jams awkwardly and he is stuck. He is still prone on the deck, facing the stern, and capsizes again in that position. What do you do?

4. You are paddling in a single kayak in the San Juan islands. With you are two friends, John and Jane, in a double. You are an intermediate paddler, John and Jane are beginners. Jane is the stronger of the two. On the first morning of this weekend trip, the double is already experiencing difficulty. John is a very weak paddler and Jane is having to do most of the work but she cannot seem to control the boat very well. You head in to shore for a lunch break. Before setting off again, you decide to switch with Jane. You take the stern

of the double and she takes your single. You start a 3 to 4 mile crossing over to the next island. Half-way across a squall comes up. The wind is fierce. The current is running 3–4kt. Jane is falling farther and farther behind. What do you do?

SOLO SEA KAYAKING

Why?

The reasons why people solo paddle are very personal but there are a number of things that are common throughout:

- Solitude: when travelling alone, the paddler can go at their own pace and focus on where they are. There is something very rewarding about a few days on the water with just a kayak, a camera and a notebook.
- Confidence: solo trips build confidence in planning, navigation and decision-making, as well as physical skills.
- Hassle free: if you are into photography or writing there is nobody to give you a hard time about shooting four rolls of one sunrise. You will see more wildlife because you are quieter and less obtrusive. If you want to go further or do less, the decision is yours.

The Flip Side

There is no doubt about it, solo expeditions are riskier and more stressful than paddling with others. There is nobody to rescue you if you capsize or get stuck on a beach for two days, and at the end of the day you have no one to share the experience with or to discuss your plans for the next day.

Do not let the following 'what ifs' scare you out of paddling alone – it is a great way to explore the sea and coast, but being prepared will hopefully keep you out of trouble.

What Ifs?

Broken paddle. Most kayakers keep their spare paddles on the back deck, where they are hard to get at. Store them on the front deck where they can be grabbed more easily. It may be worth practising flipping over, pulling out half of a spare and rolling up with it. With good technique, you can roll a loaded boat with half a paddle.

Lost hatch cover. Hatch covers usually come off because of big waves, which means the sea is pretty big already! Flooding a compartment on the water is not good when in company, let alone solo. A boat with a blown hatch can be paddled with a lot of effort if the paddler stays in the boat. If you end up swimming, water in one compartment and the cockpit will cause a 'Cleopatra's Needle' situation (kayak floating vertically with one end submerged). This is tough but rescue is possible with another boat nearby; if you are alone, then your options are very limited. Do what you can to ensure the hatches do not come off. Some hatch covers are designed with solid strapping. If the hatches do not have nylon straps with Fastex buckles, consider attaching them. This can also be done with bungie line. If you are paddling on a short trip with empty compartments, inflate some whitewater-style float bags (or even airtight dry bags) to fill the compartment.

Damaged boat. A repair kit should be a standard item for any group, so bring one when you are heading out alone.

Lost boat. Losing (or, even worse, sinking) a kayak is probably the worst outcome of a solo trip, short of bodily injury. The easiest way to end up stranded is by losing a boat from the beach. The only option then is to raise someone on the VHF or walk home. But at least you will have a tent, sleeping bag and food with you ... or will you?

A more nightmarish scenario is losing the kayak at sea. Consider if it sinks and blows away during a nasty swim, but somehow you manage to reach shore. Now you are wet, cold and without most of your gear, a tough situation for survival in remote areas. On solo trips in remote areas, dress for immersion; if you do not, you might not make that swim to shore in the first place. Keep a VHF radio in a waterproof bag in the PDF.

Carry a 'grab' bag of survival basics (a waist bag is ideal) that can be grabbed quickly, either behind the seat or on the back deck. The grab bag should have a knife, fire starter (matches and Vaseline-soaked cotton balls in a film canister), flares, some compact, high-energy food such as jerky or energy bars, a survival bag and a plastic bag for collecting water.

Tips for a Happy Trip

Start easy. Pick an area where there are likely

Expedition Kit List	
This suggested list is intended to be added to and adapted to your own needs!	
Paddling Kit	**Safety Gear**
Boat	Map and map case
Paddle and leash	Clip-on compass
Wellies/neoprene booties	VHF radio
Dry trousers	Paddle float
Cag	Towline
Hat/sun hat	First-aid kit
Pogues/gloves	Repair kit
Spray deck	Split paddles
Buoyancy aid with: Platypus hoser, flare and	Hand pump
lightstick in dry bag, whistle, compass, Paddlok key,	Emergency dry bag: para flare, pinpoint flare,
munchy bars, waterproof camera, nose clip	handsmoke, waterproof epoxy, emergency bivvy
	bag, spare VHF battery, handwarmers
Personal Kit	Paddling T-shirt
Wallet	Paddling long-sleeved top
Mobile phone	Campsite trousers, T-shirt
Headtorch/spare batteries	Underwear
Book	Fleece
Midge net	Warm hat
Sun cream	Nightwear
Sunglasses	'Bathroom' dry bag
Lip salve	Wash bag
Vaseline	Loo roll in plastic ziplock bag
'Kitchen' dry bag	Disposal bags
Stove	Travel towel
Fuel	Camping gear
Matches/lighter	Tent
Pans	Sleeping bag and liner
Tin opener/knife	Thermarest and pillow
Cutlery	Goretex bivvy bag
Plate(s) and mug	Shortwave radio
Baby wipes	'Warm' dry bag
Biodegradeable soap	Spare fleece
Tea bags/hot chocolate/cup-a-soup/coffee	Spare hat
Rubbish bags	Gloves
Clothes dry bag	Warm socks
Paddling trousers	Balaclava
Miscellaneous	**Other Gear**
Water carrier	Food
Down jacket in dry bag	Breakfast (X days +1)
Waterproof jacket and trousers	Lunch (X days +1)
Trainers/walking boots/sandals	Dinner (X days +1)
Kite/toys/games	Beer/wine
Camera in waterproof case or bag	Snacks (dried fruit, muesli bars)

to be other people around. This reduces the risk and can provide social contact and stress release. Also, do your first trip or two in an area that you are familiar with and which has relatively little objective risk.

Hone your safety skills. The consequences of a swim are much more serious when solo paddling. Add to it the possibility of the wind blowing a kayak away or a holed boat, and the situation can become very serious quickly. Good bracing and self-rescue skills are musts, and the ability to roll a loaded boat is ideal. It is likely that when you need these skills it will be when you are already tired, so practise until the skills become second nature.

Learn about yourself. Understand how you react to stress. The mental challenge can be as big or bigger than the physical one. Self-knowledge of how you will react to the stresses encountered is the difference between enjoying a trip or worrying your way through it.

Confront your fears and the solitude. Do not sit in a tent on the first night – grab a torch and go for a night walk.

Use good equipment. Know and trust your equipment. A solid spare paddle, first aid boat repair kits and flares (check their date) are all gear that hopefully you will not need – but you do need to have them with you. A VHF is advisable for solo travel.

CREATURE COMFORTS

Men and women are equal, until it comes to having a pee in a kayak, when men have a distinct advantage. If you plan to paddle on the sea where safe pullouts are hours apart, it is important to be able to relieve yourself while still in the kayak; even when it is possible to land, a quick toilet break can be an ordeal. Are you going to use toilet paper? What will you do with it afterwards, burn it or carry it out? Can leaves be used?

For men it is easy – use a pee bottle and flush it over the side. For woman it is a little more complicated, but there are several techniques available. Women can try squatting with a plastic container in the cockpit, but it is unsteady in big seas and a poor aim can have disastrous results. There are some portable urinal products designed to aid women having a pee in awkward situations: the travel mate allows females to pee through a fly hole (www.travelmateinfo.com); the 'Lady J' and 'Sanifem Freshette' are available in the USA.

A method that requires a little more co-operation from friends is to first, pull alongside a trustworthy friend and have them firmly hold onto the combing of the cockpit so that the boat is steady. Carefully stand up, turn around to face the stern and place one foot into the other kayak. Finally, squat between the boats, the spray deck will provide visual protection. When you are finished the ocean offers a perfect bidet.

EXPEDITIONING

Camping out of a kayak, like other lightweight forms of camping, can be made easier by choosing gear and techniques that make chores quick and easy. Gear that can double for a variety of tasks will keep kayaks lighter and clutter-free.

Packing a Kayak

Packing a kayak for an extended trip is a skill that takes time to perfect. Proper consideration of balance and trim will not only improve kayak performance, it will also enhance the paddler's enjoyment of the trip. For the best trim, keep light items in the bow and stern, and increase the weight of the items as you move toward the cockpit. It may be prudent to add kit or water containers to an otherwise empty sea kayak to prevent its possible 'twitchy' motion when unloaded, but follow the same principles as for packing a kayak.

An equipment list is useful (*see* Expedition Kit List) to ensure important items are not forgotten. Lay out all the gear and divide it into essential, good to have and luxury items, then decide what will fit in your boat. Remember, just because you can take the 'kitchen sink', does not mean that you should. Packing light and efficiently will make the trip much more enjoyable. Lots of small dry bags are easier to fit in the hatches than one big one.

Keep in mind what items will be required first when you land. If the paddle is a long one and it is dark on arrival, have a head-torch handy. A small first-aid kit in a deck bag is good for easy access (store a more complete kit in the boat). Everyone keeps their water bottle handy, but also remember to keep spare water handy too. If the trip has a lunch stop on the way to the next campsite, have lunch easily accessible plus a pair of windproof trousers to keep the chill off.

A kayak will achieve some extra stability and tracking ability with the addition of properly packed weight. Make sure you are aware of the manufacturer's stated weight capacity. Pack heavy gear as low as possible to keep the centre of gravity low and make sure your gear does not shift around in rough paddling conditions. All gear should be secured to prevent it rolling about in the hatches.

Front Deck

Anything on the deck will add windage (resistance to the wind) and raise your centre of

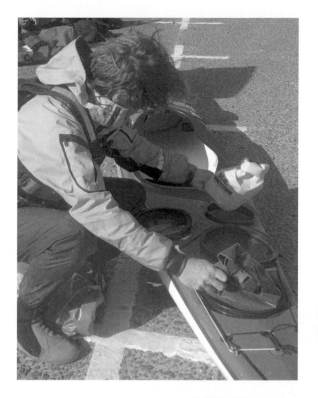

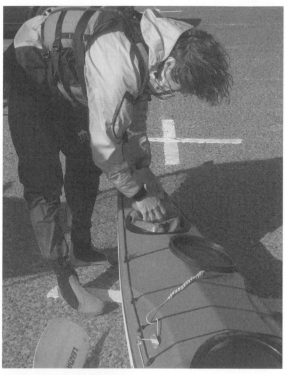

Packing a kayak.

gravity. However, and especially on long trips, some essential items need to be accessible without popping your spray deck. Essentials may include: spare paddles, water bottles, snacks, VHF radio, paddle float, sun screen and a chart. A deck bag is perfect for these and other small items. For extended voyages, strap on a small survival kit. Anything on the front or rear deck must be secured for foul conditions and surf launches or landings.

Rear Deck

We do not recommend spare paddles be placed on the rear deck because they can tangle with towlines. Do not load the front or rear deck with bags that will not fit into the kayak. Re-examine the equipment list and leave behind any unnec-

essary items. Think like a backpacker – even if there is lots of room!

Tips:

- Use water bags or bottles that collapse when the water is used up.
- Carry one or two larger bags to carry gear back and forth from the boat to the campsite. Select bags that will easily stow away when the boat is packed.
- Do not carry the kayak when it is loaded with gear.
- The new compression dry bags from Ortlieb are great for sleeping bags and clothes.
- Make equipment do double duty – sleeping pad/chair combos are good.

Suggestions for Packing a Kayak with Three Hatches	
Front Hatch Thermarest (stuff sack) Food and drink Eating utensils (Tupperware) Cooking utensils Spice kit Dishwashing stuff Cup and bowl Garbage bags Stove and fuel (dry bag) Carrying bag First-aid kit	**Front Deck** Chart Compass Pump Water bottle VHF radio Spare paddles
Back Hatch Clothing bag (dry bag) Books and paper (dry bag) Repair kit (dry bag) Water container (self contained) Tent and poles (self contained) Sleeping bag and night gear (dry bag) Rain gear (stuff sack) Hiking shoes (stuff sack)	**PFD** Whistle Energy food Sunscreen Binoculars Waterproof watch Flares
Third Cockpit or On The Deck Pee bottle Emergency grab bag (attached to you in rough conditions) 15m throw line (attached to seat) Sponge Mobile phone VHF radio Paddlefloat Towline Pump **NB** Ensure everything is tied down, so you do not lose it all should you come out of your kayak	

Camping on a beach.

- Keep your dry top handy in case of sudden storms.

Tents and Camping

Choosing a campsite is an important decision for comfort and enjoyment of the trip. A sandy beach with limitless sky and fresh water and bug-free is a delight.

Pitching tents in a shoreline environment can pose some challenges because you may be dealing with anything from loose dry sand to good-sized rocks. When tent pegs prove inadequate for the task and driftwood is not available, use the rest of the gear to help – a bilge pump or spare paddle can be wedged into the sand and serve as anchor points. Stuff sacks and dry bags can be filled with stones and used as tie-down points or placed inside the corners of the tent body to anchor it against the wind. Likewise,

kayak grab handles and deck lines can be used as guyline points if needed.

Tents are awkward bundles to pack into the openings of some sea kayaks. If so, pack the tent components in separate stuff sacks. The rigid pole bag will often fit alongside the seat in the cockpit or on the deck, but beware – aluminium alloys are corroded by sea water, so rinse them well afterwards.

There are a huge variety of tents on the market from the super cheap to the ultra expensive and from the very tiny to the enormous. Top of the range tents are often designed for extreme camping on mountains and the cheaper end of the market will often suffice for camping close to the sea. Tents where the inner tent contains the pole will provide more space and less guying. The fact that the inner can get wet when it is raining is not a problem. Tents with flexible poles are easier to pitch on sand and require

An MSR stove.

little guying. Unless space is at a premium in your kayak, buy a tent that is roomy.

There is also the minimalistic way of camping by using a tarp – a simple length of weatherproof fabric with a selection of eyelets around the edges. Use a kayak to anchor the windward side and two paddles as poles, along with adequate guylines and hey presto – a shelter. Extra kayaks can form a wind break. The tarp has the advantage that it can also be used as a sail.

Sleeping Bags
Choice of sleeping bag will be affected by how a person feels the cold, as well as its intended use. Sleeping bags are 'comfort rated' for a certain temperature. This is obviously a very subjective thing, since metabolism rate and tolerance of cold may vary from the 'norm'. Women are often said to 'sleep colder' (prefer more insulation) than men. The bag is one of the bulkiest items to go into the boat. Older, synthetic-insulated bags pack much larger than down bags of similar

warmth, but newer fibre fillings seem to compress more easily. Even when a down bag is kept out of the rain, it is likely to become damp from perspiration and is less effective if used during cool, humid weather. Contrary to popular belief, they are not a nightmare to dry out, especially when the weather is dry. However, since synthetics are less expensive and easier to care for and retain warmth when wet, the small difference in size is not worth the risk of a bad night's sleep.

Sleeping Mats
A Thermarest or other compact sleeping mat will make the difference between a good night's sleep and a painful ordeal, and is generally considered essential equipment by all but the most hardened campers. A good sleeping mat will add a few degrees to the warmth of a sleeping bag, in addition to adding comfort. The thinner versions are usually sufficient and the three-quarter length designs save some bulk and

cost less than a full-length pad. Closed-cell foam is much cheaper than the inflatable Thermarest type, but takes up more valuable space in the boat and is not quite as plush but it also cannot be punctured. A camping-size pillow is also nice to have, but is not nearly as important as a sleeping mat and it is easy to fill a jumper or fleece with clothes to make a pillow.

Stoves

Cooking on a kayak trip poses some unique issues. If convenient tables or logs are unavailable, a kayak might be the best sand-free surface for miscellaneous camp chores. If it is windy, the inside of the cockpit or stern compartment can act as an effective windscreen and provide a stable surface for the stove.

Gasoline stoves are best for extended camping, with MSR being our favourite and the most reliable. Trangia alcohol stoves are light and simple in design, but they are hard to regulate, do not get as hot and burn much more fuel, so the weight advantage disappears after a couple of meals, since you have to carry pounds of alcohol. Gas is clean and easy to use but expensive. One stove per small group is adequate, but two is a cheap luxury.

Campfires

Of all the things humans do in the wild, the campfire is one of the most destructive but also one of the fundamental things we all enjoy. It is possible to have a fire without leaving any evidence that there has been one! That means using the inter-tidal zone so that the remains of the fire are washed away on the tide. In the morning, remove all traces and kick the sand over the fire pit.

If you really, really have to build a fire on a grassy area, remove the turf, line the edges with stones and clear the ashes when cold before replacing the turf. The ground will recover in a

Scarring due to a camp fire.

couple of weeks. If you cannot remove the turf, use stones to make a fire ring and fill the centre with about 15cm (6in) of sand. Build the fire on that to protect the ground underneath. On leaving, scatter the ashes, remove the stones and clear the sand back on to the beach. Please consider whether a fire should be lit if you cannot protect the grass or fragile machair. Whatever method you use, remember to water the area well – fires can, and do, spontaneously re-ignite. There is no need for large fires, leave some wood for the next campers. If you come across damage from others' poor practice, remove the stones and ashes and roughen the surface of the burned area to help the grass re-establish.

Think about the fuel as well. Driftwood is good but wood from fresh trees does not burn well and is damaging. There is a sea-paddler active in Scotland who is known to just buy a bag of logs on his way to the coast and take that with him.

A note of caution – think about what you are burning. Most treated wood, e.g. a fence-post washed up on the beach, contains arsenic and burning PVC creates a serious hazard in that particulates (smoke) containing toxic and persistent dioxins are produced, due to the chlorine content of the material.

Finally, be wary of lighting a fire on peat or heather when it has been really dry – there is a risk of the fire smouldering under the surface, which can travel a surprisingly long way and burst to life again after you have left.

Cooking Gear

Bring at least one more pot than stoves, because you will probably want to make a brew while making a meal or some such combination. Non-stick surfaces are nice, but are damaged when cleaning and transporting them. Pack each nested pot inside a plastic grocery bag, or the bigger pot outside it will get scratched. Bring a couple of extra grocery bags for garbage. Choose cooksets that use a pliers-type handle that can be used for all the pots. The MSR design is good, but some brands are flimsy or tricky to use, so beware.

Getting Clean Water

The water in lakes or rivers in developing countries should always be considered unclean, but the concentration of bugs is usually low enough for your stomach acid to deal with small volumes of water (such as from splashes). In countries with seasonal monsoons, the rivers are most contaminated immediately after the rains start, when the land gets 'flushed'.

Prior to purification, remove any suspended particulate and organic matter; this improves the effectiveness of purification and often the taste. The low-tech method is to let the water stand for at least one hour and then remove the clear surface water without disturbing the sediment by dipping or pouring through a coffee filter. A faster method, and one that removes material that will not settle with simple gravity, is to add ⅛ to ¼ tsp/gal of aluminum sulphate (alum), mix thoroughly, and then wait for five minutes, stirring occasionally. When the floc has settled, decant the clear water from the surface. Alum can be found in the spice section of some specialist food stores (alum is also known as pickling powder).

BOILING

As long as the water exceeds 86°C, bugs are killed. Since the temperature of boiled water (even at altitude) exceeds 86°C and the time necessary to bring it to the boil (even at altitude) exceeds a few minutes, water brought to the boil is safe. Since taste comes from both the oxygen and mineral content of the water, the flat taste of boiled water may be improved by pouring it from container to container for a few minutes. Clearly the advantage of boiling is its effectiveness. The disadvantages are the availability of fuel and the amount of time required to bring the water to a boil.

FILTERS

Filters are effective against protozoans, bacteria and parasites, if their pore size is small enough (Giardia and amoeba cysts: 5 microns; most enteric bacteria: 0.2–5 microns, Cryptosporidium: less than 3 microns, and general parasite eggs and larvae: 20–30 microns). Filters that use an iodine resin may give some protection against viruses; however, because contact time is short, they are not completely reliable. The advantage to filters is their high speed and reasonably good taste. The major disadvantage is that they do not offer reliable protection against viruses.

IODINE

Iodine is effective against viruses, bacteria and protozoans, except Cryptosporidium cysts. It is available in tablet, liquid, crystals or resin form.

A water pump.

Pregnant women, persons taking lithium and those with a known iodine allergy or with an active thyroid problem, should not use it. In addition, iodine use should be limited to months of continued use rather than years.

Contact with organic material renders iodine inactive, prefiltering (clarification) is required if the water is cloudy (*see* above). The effectiveness of iodine depends on three criteria: the temperature of the water, the concentration of the halogen and the contact time. Contact time is shorter with warm water and longer with cold water; it takes much longer to kill *Giardia* cysts in very cold water.

The advantages of iodine are that it is easy to carry and fast to use. Poor taste can be eliminated by adding a small amount of powdered ascorbic acid (vitamin C) to the water after it has been treated (not at the same time!) to mop up any iodine.

If fuel and time are readily available, choose boiling – especially if you have the means to safely store and carry the treated water. Filters work well at altitude or in snow country where the chance of viral infection is minimal and *Giardia* may be present (as in snow melt or old snow; fresh snow is usually safe). Iodine works well if you are able to use it and if there is no risk of *Cryptosporidium*. Most people use a combination of methods depending on how and where they are travelling. I have successfully used all of the above methods during my outdoor career. I tend to rely on boiling water when in camp and iodine while travelling. Remember to clarify all cloudy water before purification.

Food

Food is a very personal thing and some people cannot stand cooking, while many are just lazy. Remember any fool can be uncomfortable but it does not take much effort to turn a simple meal into a culinary delight.

PLANNING

It is easy for paddlers to dehydrate, so everyone should drink at least 2 litres of water per day. Salads, fruits and vegetables also help to hydrate and replace electrolytes. As long as you have a varied diet and are not pushing very hard day after day to your limits, electrolyte/sports drinks are not needed, as the electrolytes will be replaced through your food. Most packaged foods are salty enough, so discourage salty snacks and encourage everyone to drink lots of water while paddling and at snack time. The greater the variety of food eaten, the better is the chance that you will have of getting the more than fifty nutrients the body needs each day. Develop a menu with a day by day ingredient list that turns into a shopping and packing plan. Look up recipes from your favourite cookbooks. Here are some tips to make you think about what you could eat:

- Take fresh fruit and vegetables from local farm markets – apart from helping the local economies, they are going to be fresher and last longer. The meals will also be more palatable.
- Check dairy items for expiry date. On a trip, use milk, cottage and cream cheese within the first two to three days. Yoghurt can last a week; cheese longer.

- Fresh meat, fish and poultry last a day or two; eggs a week and even longer if you coat them with grease or wrap them in cling film.
- Dried meats work for longer trips. Salami sausage keeps up to five days in summer conditions. Heat up slivers of salami to put into fajitas.
- Beans such as pinto, soy, chickpeas and lentils are nutritional powerhouses.
- Nuts are a great alternative to meat. Almonds and cashews are preferable, since peanuts and walnuts tend to go rancid in the heat. Bring along a variety of seeds (sesame, sunflower, pumpkin) to toss into salads and main dishes; and butters (peanut, almond, cashew, soy nut or sesame tahini).
- Textured vegetable proteins (TVP) in soups and curries will fool most people. Textured vegetable proteins can simulate ground beef or chunks of meat – look for them in health food stores.
- Choose dark breads such as rye – they can stay edible for a week or so.
- Think about baking your own quick breads – it is not as hard as you imagine and can be great fun.
- Bring along spices in small zip-lock bags or small plastic bottles with screw tops: salt, pepper, garlic flakes and an all spice mix – equal parts of seasoned salt, oregano and marjoram, plus a dash of thyme and a dash of onion powder in a bag.
- Choose high-fibre, energy-rich snacks such as dates, figs, low-fat grain bars, trail mix and prunes.
- Bring extra crackers and snacks, with enough for an extra dinner in case of delays.
- Make your own mixes – hot cereals, pancake mixes, scone mixes. It is cheaper and gives control over the quality of the ingredients.
- Calculate the number of servings based on the number of paddlers. You will probably average two and a half slices of bread for each person – so twenty slices for a group of eight.
- Write in the amounts from recipes but expect a recipe for six to serve four after a day's paddling.

PRESENTATION

People eat twice – first with their eyes. Bring parsley in a yoghurt container with holes punched in the lid. Look around camp to see what you can add to a meal. Chop wild onions into main courses and add the onion flowers to

Food is very important!

salads. Sea asparagus or beach peas can be a surprise vegetable. Pick whatever berries are in season and a sprig of wild mint to dress up food.

PACKING

- Discard outer packaging but keep the instructions and repack them into freezer-weight zip-lock plastic bags. Group foods together in a larger zip-lock.
- Use a colour-coding system that works for you; for example, orange or yellow for breakfasts (sunrise); blue (like the sky) for lunch; red for sunsets and dinners; black for coffee, tea and hot chocolate.
- Pack cheeses and butter in a separate bag or soft-sided cooler bag and keep them near the bottom of the hull.
- Keep food away from fuels, toiletries, soaps and other odour pollutants. Keep foods with strong smells separate. Do not store coffee

with other foods and keep peppermint separate from other teas.
- Plan the packing so you know where everything is or who has what.
- Protect soft fruits and vegetables by packing them in round plastic containers that can then become your salad or mixing bowls. After you have eaten the produce, use any spare containers for rubbish. Or you can pack soft fruits and veggies on top of the gear before closing the hatch cover.

REMOTE FIRST AID FOR PADDLERS

One of the pleasures of sea kayaking is reaching beautiful and remote places; this does however mean that a sea paddler should be ready to rely on his or her own knowledge and resources. The commonest accidents on kayak trips are caused by foolishness or lack of foresight – campfire

First-aid kit.

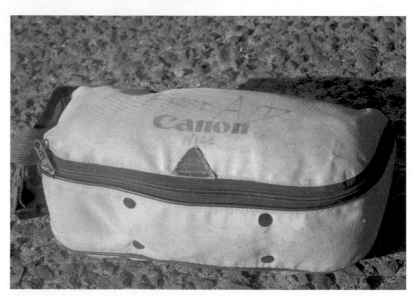

burns, twisted ankles due to inadequate foot-wear and so on – rather than natural incidents.

Any sea paddler should know basic life support including cardiopulmonary resuscitation (CPR), because lightning strikes, near drownings, chokings and cardiac arrests can and do occur in outdoor settings. Many trips require nothing more than a minimal knowledge of first aid, but longer more remote expeditions should not be undertaken unless there is someone along with more formal training in outdoor emergency care.

There is no way that a short section in this book can to do justice to first aid; a Rescue and Emergency Care (REC) course or similar is an essential starting point. This section is simply an eclectic look at common acute injuries that can create serious problems whilst kayaking, as opposed to overuse or chronic irritation such as tendinitis, bursitis and delayed-onset muscle soreness.

The most important resource a paddler has in dealing with an outdoor emergency is their brain. Having a plan of action when things start to go wrong is essential. Prepare yourself by imagining how you would like to cope in a crisis.

- Stay calm – running round like a headless chicken helps nobody.
- Make an accurate assessment of the situation.
- Avoid making rash decisions with incomplete information.
- Establish a plan that will resolve the situation as quickly and efficiently as possible. Many crises go from bad to worse quickly because of poor decision-making.
- Do not forget the rest of the group if you are leading.

Note: The authors are not medically trained and the information given below is meant to augment your knowledge gained from a first-aid training course, not to replace the need for a first-aid course. If you have any doubt about a course of action, do not do it!

A Possible/Near Drowning

Dealing with a potential drowning incident is not only a life-saving issue but a life-threatening one for the rescuer. A drowning person should be reached with a paddle, the end of a boat or a throw line. A swimming rescue is a last resort, because the victim may grab the rescuer. Near-drowning ranges from a bad swim with a gasping but conscious victim, to prolonged immersion with loss of consciousness. This can be 'dry drowning' where the larynx or voice box closes in spasm, thereby preventing both air and water getting to the lungs. It is more common in cold water. The victim should be assessed for consciousness, respiration and pulse. A quick assessment should be done to see if the person has a head or neck trauma. If an unconscious patient is not breathing, rescue breathing should be initiated. Efforts to remove water from the lungs are not usually successful. Giving ventilation as quickly as possible will most likely aid in a drowning victim's survival. If the patient has no pulse, perform chest compressions in accordance with CPR guidelines. Once the person has recovered, medical treatment should be sought as soon as possible.

If the patient has suffered prolonged immersion at sea, they should be lifted out horizontally (to stop the blood pressure dropping severely) and gently, especially if they are hypothermic –

rough handling has been known to induce fatal rhythms in a hypothermic heart.

Head injuries may be a cause of unconsciousness and are often accompanied by neck injuries. Removal of a helmet should be done by two people, with one responsible for holding the head stable. If a neck injury is suspected, remember that establishing the airway means lifting the chin, not bending the neck.

Management of a near drowned casualty:

- place in the recovery position – the victim is likely to vomit;
- keep the victim warm, move as little as possible;
- start regular observations of respiratory and pulse rate, temperature and, if possible, urine output.

Severe respiratory illness ('secondary drowning') is heralded by breathlessness and the patient looks very unwell. It occurs 12–24h after a near-drowning and is more likely if the near-drowning was severe; for example with unconsciousness, or if 'crackles' can be heard when you put your ear to the patient's chest. In the wilderness, there is no difference in the management of near-drowning in salt or fresh water.

Wounds and Lacerations

Wounds and lacerations at sea are rarely serious, but wounds managed improperly can lead to life- or limb-threatening complications. Everyone engaged in outdoor activities should have an up-to-date tetanus booster, because bacteria are everywhere and once a laceration occurs they are in the wound.

When assessing a wound or laceration always suspect a fracture of the underlying bone or a laceration of nerve, vessel, muscle or tendon. If these associated injuries are present, they should not be dealt with in the field but should be temporarily stabilized and the wounded person transported to a hospital. When stabilizing any wound, control bleeding (even heavy bleeding from severed arteries) by holding direct pressure on the wound and elevating the limb if possible. Abrasions should be thoroughly cleansed using soap and water, then treated with an application of a topical antibiotic ointment and a clean or sterile dressing. Superficial lacerations should be irrigated with sterile saline solution and can be closed with adhesive strips that are provided in many medical kits. If a laceration is deep, with exposed muscle, tendon or deep fat, then closure in the wilderness entails the risk of trapping bacteria deep in the wound, which can cause abscess formation. These wounds should be irrigated with sterile saline solution and packed open with sterile dressings until medical attention can be reached.

Sprains and Strains

Sprains and strains are common injuries. A sprain is an injury to a ligament that connects bone to bone.

- A sprain can range from microscopic tearing to complete disruption of the ligament. In assessing these injuries, check for tenderness over the ligament and instability of the joint. This may indicate a complete disruption.
- A strain is an injury that occurs where a muscle attaches to the tendon. These injuries can also range from microscopic tearing to complete disruption of the muscle tendon junction, with extensive bleeding, pain and functional loss.

In the wilderness, most sprains and strains are not cause for alarm. Although these injuries may cause discomfort and some functional impairment, they can be treated with ice, compressive wraps and elevation, if possible. It is not necessary to limit the trip, and medical treatment can be sought at a later date.

Fractures and Dislocations

Ankle fractures or shoulder dislocations are common injuries. The principles that apply to their care can be generalized to other joints as well.

If a fracture or dislocation is suspected, a thorough assessment should be performed before any treatment is given. Check pulses, feeling and movement of the hand for a shoulder injury, or the foot for an ankle injury. This includes feeling the pulse in the hand and foot of the injured extremity. Feel the radial pulse at the wrist and feel the pulse in the ankle. Test for feeling and movement in the fingers and toes. It is often difficult to distinguish a strained or sprained ankle from a broken one – if in doubt, assume it is broken.

Many fractures or dislocations will be apparent because of the gross deformity of the extremity. Other indicators will be severe pain, a sensation of crunching, bruising that is rapidly apparent, or significant swelling. The general principles of fracture and dislocation management in the wilderness are to reduce the deformity or dislocation if possible, to immobilize in order to prevent further injury and to transport to a location where definitive treatment can be obtained. To reduce a dislocated joint or fracture, one should gently correct any gross deformity and then splint the extremity. A padded ankle splint can be made with a fleece shirt and a PFD. The shoulder can be immobilized by placing the injured arm inside a PFD, or by folding the arm under a shirt.

Shoulder Dislocation

This is probably the most serious injury that sea paddlers will experience. Your future in kayaking is limited if you have a dislocation, as subsequent dislocations happen a lot more easily. Dislocations occur when the arm is extended higher than the shoulder. The diagnosis is usually obvious and patients realize the shoulder is 'out': the elbow will lie away from their side and they cannot move their arm. From the front, the shoulder looks abnormally square compared with the other side, and the head of the upper arm bone (humerus) can usually be felt in front of the 'cup' of the joint

In the wilderness, it is reasonable to try to put back ('reduce') a dislocated shoulder. Relocation can most easily be done in the first few minutes, but becomes progressively more difficult during the next two hours as muscle spasm sets in. The technique is simple, you are unlikely to cause more damage than has already been done, the healing process can start sooner, there is likely to be less damage to the shoulder in the long term and the patient will be more comfortable during the evacuation. Before embarking on a remote trip, ask a friendly doctor to show you how.

Stings and Bites

Stings and bites come from many sources. Bee stings, although not dangerous in most cases, can be potentially lethal in the 1 per cent of the population who have a hypersensitivity reaction. Anyone who has a known hypersensitivity reaction, characterized by hives, significant swelling and breathing problems, should always travel with an injectable form of epinephrine.

The general procedure when a snakebite occurs in the backcountry is to provide calm but efficient transport to a hospital as soon as possible.

Hypothermia

Hypothermia is the lowering of the body's core temperature. Water conducts heat away at twenty to twenty-five times the rate that air removes heat; this is one reason why an exposure to cold water at a certain temperature is more traumatic than exposure to air at the same temperature. Cold climates, cold water and wet clothing all lead to lower body temperatures while paddling.

Prevention is better than cure:

- Most kayakers that get hypothermia did not expect to end up in the water – wear clothing that is appropriate for immersion in the water and not the air temperature.
- Eat properly to keep your energy levels up, get enough rest and drink enough water to maintain proper hydration.
- Fatigue and dehydration help to induce hypothermia when exposed to cold.

Remember that extremely cold water can cause your hands to become useless in a relatively short time (less than 20min) even while properly dressed. This will complicate operating a pump, pulling on a spray skirt, firing off flares, radioing for help and so on. This may result in your inability to signal for help, do a self-rescue or assist in your rescue or the rescue of others.

Exposure to cold does not automatically induce hypothermia, it typically will take time to develop unless there is exposure to very cold water or there is no protection (wetsuit/drysuit) against the cold. Sometimes a person will not know they are hypothermic, since people typically do not notice it in themselves. It is important for people in a group to keep an eye on their companions for signs of hypothermia (this includes group leaders and guides). Sometimes a person will appear physically and mentally okay and will refuse treatment because they claim they are okay.

How Can You Tell if Somebody is Hypothermic?
It can be difficult to tell if someone is hypothermic without actually measuring their core temperature. Measuring a person's core temperature requires a rectal thermometer and is not often done in the field! Therefore symptoms must be relied on. Hypothermia affects people in different ways and no one symptom is reliable to indicate if a person is hypothermic. Note the following warning signs.

- Feeling cold.
- Uncontrolled shivering does mean you are hypothermic.
- A lack of shivering does not mean you are not hypothermic, since a symptom of severe hypothermia (core temperature less than 32°C) is the lack of shivering.
- Mild shivering and cold hands/feet does not indicate you are severely hypothermic. These signs do mean you are losing more heat than you are producing, and your body is adjusting its temperature. Shivering is one way your body produces heat to warm itself.
- Cold hands and feet indicate your body is fighting the cold by reducing the flow of blood to the extremities. Reduced blood flow to the extremities helps to reduce heat loss and helps maintain the body's core temperature.
- Muscles are stiff, weak and less responsive – this can lead to capsizes, failure to roll, inability to climb on to the bank.
- Mental disorientation, inappropriate behaviour and slurred speech. Accidents then become inevitable.
- Armpit feels 'marble cold'.

Mild hypothermia (core temperature from 32 to 35°C): the patient may shiver uncontrollably, experience a loss of co-ordination, stumble or slur words. For mild hypothermia, put the patient in dry clothes and protect him or her from the elements and further heat loss. Other heat sources such as a fire can be helpful.

Severe hypothermia (core temperature below 32°C): the patient may experience a further deterioration of mental status to unresponsiveness. The trunk will feel cold to the touch and the body may be rigid. In severe cases, pulse and respiration may be absent, but the patient should not be considered dead until rewarming has been accomplished.

Management of Hypothermia
Stop and warm the person up. If it is the end of the day and you are close to your destination, with no ideal campsite, the temptation is to

press on, but remember that the hypothermic person (and probably others in the group) will be markedly less competent at paddling.

- Get the patient into dry clothes (sea kayaks especially should have these accessible) and put on a hat.
- Place the patient in a sleeping bag. Putting an extra person in the sleeping bag may not be as beneficial as was previously thought.
- Insulate the patient from ground.
- Rewarm the patient.
- Give small, frequent amounts of warm fluids.
- Make the patient rest for a day after recovery.

Remember that the skin warms up before the inner (core) temperature, so early on the person feels inappropriately better. Allow plenty of time for rewarming. A person with severe hypothermia needs to get to a hospital as soon as possible. They should be considered a stretcher case and handled very carefully. Rough handling can induce an irregular heartbeat that can kill them. If they cannot be taken right away, then treat them like you would somebody with mild hypothermia. The one thing that will not help them is exercise, because at this stage they have depleted their energy reserves so much that they cannot even shiver. Exercise may even kill them by inducing an irregular heartbeat.

Unfortunately, in remote areas, not much more can be done to rewarm them beyond the measures outlined above.

Cold Shock

Cold shock is not hypothermia but it is caused by sudden immersion in cold water. It is an involuntary gasp reflex followed by hyperventilation. Typically, there is one gasp reflex. The hyperventilation can last 10–15min.

Cold shock can complicate a rescue. The gasp reflex can reduce a paddler's ability to roll due to the involuntary breathing in of water. The hyperventilation will prevent a person from holding their breath for very long, complicating the ability to do a re-entry and roll. The hyperventilation can also cause panic in some people due to the inability to breathe properly and/or the breathing in of water in rough seas.

Blisters

Blisters are common on the thumbs and pads of the fingers where the paddle rubs against the skin. Water softens hands and sand gets caught in these areas making the friction worse. Friction and pressure with the kayak and excessive moisture from sweat and damp clothing can also cause blisters on the lower back, armpits, hips, bum, knees and heels. If improperly treated, these blisters can become a trip-ending problem.

Prevention

- Reduce friction and pressure – use proper technique when paddling. Hold the paddle loosely in both hands – enlarging the shaft diameter with a fingerboard may encourage a looser grip. Trim and smooth any rough edges on the paddle shaft.
- Develop and maintain tougher skin by training regularly to build calluses. Alternatively, rub your palms with rubbing alcohol regularly prior to the start of your trip.
- Prevent blisters in novices by taping their hands before the trip begins. Use a slippery tape so the paddle can still be used correctly and do not apply just a little piece of tape, it will ruck up and make the situation worse.
- Ensure clothing and equipment fits well; minimize ridges, seams and zippers along areas of friction and pressure such as the back, armpits, hips and bum.
- Keep warm and dry. Moisture contributes to blisters by softening the skin and increasing friction. To keep moisture away from skin, wear proper layers of technical clothing. If you wear a wetsuit for long periods, wash and dry the underlying skin regularly and try to rinse and dry the wetsuit every few days.
- Wear proper-fitting gloves or pogues to help keep hands warm and dry (or at least not soaking wet).
- Dry hands and body thoroughly at rest stops, lunch and especially at night. Consider using talcum powder or antiperspirant in armpits and groin to reduce moisture build-up.

Treatment
Monitor common problem areas for early signs and symptoms of blisters. There are three stages of blister development, and the earlier they are noticed and treated, the better.

1. Red, irritated skin – cover the affected area with non-adhesive padding such as Spenco Skin Care Pad, Dura Gel or 2nd Skin. Then tape with a micropore tape or a water-proof/breathable tape. Reduce friction and pressure and keep the area dry.
2. Intact blister with trapped fluid – a blister with trapped fluid is called a 'bleb'. Leave a bleb intact unless it is too painful or awkward. Make a doughnut to pad around the bleb with non-adhesive foam or ProWrap. Then pad and tape the bleb and doughnut as in stage one. If you do have to burst a blister:

- keep it clean – wash your hands and the affected area thoroughly;
- sterilize a thin needle with alcohol or a flame (the carbon left on the needle from the flame is sterile);
- penetrate the blister from underneath through the healthy skin surrounding the blister, not through the dead skin covering the bleb;
- treat as a stage three blister, but leave the bleb skin intact to reduce the likelihood of infection.

3. Broken blister. A broken blister is an open wound, susceptible to infection. Treat as follows:

- wash your hands and the affected area thoroughly;
- remove the dead skin with a sterile dispos-able scalpel or sterilized scissors;
- remove any debris by soaking in warm, sterile water or by irrigating with a large-gauge syringe or a bag with a hole;
- cover the blister with sterile, impregnated gauze that will not stick to the wound;
- pad the blister with sterile gel, such as sterile 2nd Skin; if the area is exception-ally painful, surround the wound with a doughnut as in stage two;
- tape the area as in stage one, using sterile waterproof/breathable tape.

Sunburn

Skin cancer is the most common form of cancer! But cancer is not the only effect of the sun's UV rays. Frequent exposure to the sun also causes roughening, thinning and wrinkling of the skin,

broken blood vessels, sallow or dry skin on the face and liver spots on the backs of hands. Eyes are also in danger. Cataracts, pterygium (a fleshy growth that forms on the white of your eyes then invades the cornea) and pingueculum (a yellow patch or bump on the white of your eyes) have all been linked to UV ray exposure.

UV rays are divided into three categories according to the frequency of their wavelength. UVA have the slowest frequency and penetrate to the deepest layers of the skin. They cause tanning and burning, wrinkling, premature ageing of the skin and are potentially carcino-genic. UVB rays have a higher frequency and are stopped short at the skin's surface where they are believed to damage the skin's immune system, which can ultimately result in cancer. UVB rays also cause sunburn and skin ageing. The highest frequency UVC rays are absorbed by the ozone layer in the upper atmosphere – for now anyway.

Protecting the body from the disastrous effects of UV rays is simple. Create shade by wearing a wide brimmed hat and sunglasses that provide 100 per cent protection from both UVA and UVB rays. Use sunscreen with a minimum SPF (sun protection factor) of 15 and wear protective clothing. Use a sunblock, such as zinc oxide, talc or titanium dioxide, that literally blocks out the sun's rays. These products are especially good for nose, lips and people with fair skin. Both sunscreens and sunblocks should be used in conjunction with hats, sunglasses and protective clothing. They provide additional protection, not a ticket to bask in the sun for hours on end. Lips are particularly vulnerable to the harmful effects of the sun because lips lack melatonin, the skin's natural shield against the sun.

The higher the composition of synthetic fibres, the tighter the weave of the fabric and darker colours will provide better protection. A new, white, cotton T-shirt, for example, provides a SPF of 7 but a dark blue, polypropylene, long sleeved shirt may provide an SPF many times that. For a simple test at home, hold up your clothes in front of a light. The more light visible through the fabric, the more ultraviolet light will also get through.

As for sunglasses, the chemical added to the lenses of sunglasses to block out UV light is inexpensive. Therefore, a good pair of sunglasses do not have to break the bank. As long as they have an even shading of grey, brown or green, quality ground lenses to prevent eyestrain and a rating for UVA and UVB protection, the sunglasses will protect your eyes.

Remember that up to 80 per cent of the sun's rays can penetrate through cloud cover and are reflected off water. Paddlers should therefore take the same precautions on a cloudy day that they do on a sunny day.

Finally, check your skin regularly for changes in moles, sores that do not heal and the development of irregularly shaped or oddly coloured spots (especially those larger that the top of a pencil eraser). If any of these problems develop, seek advice from your doctor.

Dehydration

A 5 per cent drop in hydration levels can reduce performance by up to 50 per cent. Paradoxically, despite being surrounded by water, dehydration can be a problem, especially for sea paddlers in hot areas, who may not realize that water intake in the sun should be about 2 to 3 litres a day. The early signs of dehydration are vague symptoms such as headache, light-headedness, lethargy and just feeling unwell.

Diarrhoea

If anyone in the group gets diarrhoea, tighten up on hygiene practices. Treatment for simple diarrhoea for the first few days is fluid replacement, not medicines. If the diarrhoea is accompanied by abdominal pain, blood or fever, or persists for more than one to two days, antibiotics, such as ciprofloxacin, may be considered.

Colds, Earache and Sore Throats

These are fairly common on multi-day trips. Treatment is simple, with paracetamol and plenty of fluids. If the infection moves down to the chest, purulent (green) sputum can result. Anything worse than this should probably be treated with antibiotics (amoxycillin or erythromycin), especially if the patient has a temperature. Kayakers sometimes complain of 'water in the ear', often when they have a cold and have been rolling. The sensation is in fact not caused by water in the external ear but by an imbalance of pressure in the inner ear caused by a blockage of the very narrow tube that joins the inner ear to the throat (Eustachian tube). This pressure may be eased by exhaling against a closed mouth and pinched nose, or by swallowing. Inhaling steam may help, or try decongestants such as Actifed. You should wait until any colds have cleared before going back to Eskimo rolls, and it can be painful during the descent of a plane flight.

External Ear Infections

External ear infections are common in warm, moist areas such as the tropics. Encourage expedition members to carefully wash and dry the ear, then use Otosporin ear drops (two drops three times a day). On the water, you may want to try an earplug of cotton wool in Vaseline. If you already suffer from 'surfer's ear' (exostoses or bony lumps, caused by years of exposure to cold water), you should discuss a plan for its treatment with your doctor.

EVACUATION

When to Call for Help?

Severe injuries in the wild mean help must be called immediately, either by radio or phone, or by sending someone from the group for help. In these situations, time is truly of the essence and can make the difference between a favourable outcome and a disastrous one.

Head injuries can result in uncontrolled swelling of the brain within the skull. If a person has a concussion that lasts longer than one to two minutes, significant facial trauma, a severe headache, altered mental status, or nausea and vomiting, then evacuation should be sought.

Any spinal injury that results in significant localized pain or tenderness of the neck or back should be presumed to be an unstable injury until proven otherwise. Obvious signs of injury, such as loss of muscle strength in the arms or legs or loss of sensation, can be ominous. Ideally, someone with medical training should examine the patient. The mechanism of injury can give a clue as to whether a spinal injury is likely. Diving into shallow water, a fall from significant height or high-speed deceleration (landing flat after paddling over a waterfall) can result in spinal injuries. In these situations, the patient should be placed flat and log-rolled until they can be evaluated by medical personnel, because attempted transport by those untrained can lead to neurologic injury. Evacuation may be necessary.

Open fractures are where the bone penetrates the skin exposing the bone to contamination. Pressure dressings should be placed to keep the bone ends clean, and any gross deformity should be minimized and splinted, if possible. Transport time is critical to reduce the risk of infection. Patients should be quickly moved by ground or air transport to the nearest medical centre.

Medical Kits

What to take in a medical kit is a controversial topic. The size and contents of a kit will vary with the length and location of the trip, as well as the level of sophistication of the personnel on the trip. Medical kits can be divided into three categories:

- day trips, where medical care is relatively easily accessible;
- multi-day trips, where greater self-reliance is necessary,
- expeditions.

For day trips, a medical kit should contain basic wound cleansing and covering materials, such as hydrogen peroxide, an antibiotic ointment, gauze and tape. Band-aids and blister-prevention materials, such as moleskin, are also helpful. This is an 'ouch pouch', assembled with the assumption that more sophisticated care can be delivered elsewhere. For multi-day trips, increase your preparedness. In addition to the above, consider butterfly-type closure strips for wound closure, saline bags to irrigate wounds and a snakebite kit. Local anaesthetic and suture material are nice if there is someone with experience available. A prefabricated orthopaedic splint and ace wrap should be included. An injectable epinephrine-dose syringe should be carried. Remember, include what is likely to be useful and leave out what seems superfluous. Although it is good to be prepared, large and cumbersome medical kits are likely to be left behind. With expedition trips, the list can become exhaustive but your local doctor should be able to help.

In summary, the majority of outdoor mishaps can be taken care of with relatively little in the way of preparation and supplies. Sprains, strains, abrasions, contusions and lacerations are by far the most common injuries. With a basic medical kit and some knowledge, you can handle most things as they arise and enjoy paddling even though there is no casualty.

APPENDIX

NATIONAL AND INTERNATIONAL ASSOCIATIONS AND ORGANIZATIONS

www.acanet.org The American Canoe Association

www.bcu.org.uk Home of the governing body for the sport and recreation of canoeing (kayaking) in the United Kingdom.

www.canoe.org.au Australian Canoeing

www.gasp-seakayak.org Club for paddlers in the Gulf of Mexico, from Texas to Florida, and the Caribbean area. Trip reports, FAQ, articles, fun stuff and more.

www.geocities.com/Yosemite/Gorge/4657 Great Lakes Sea Kayaking Association.

www.iol.ie Irish Sea Kayaking Association.

www.kask.co.nz Kiwi Association of Sea Kayakers

www.qajaqusa.org Greenland Kayak Association

www.rivers.org.nz/nzrca The national organization responsible for the sport and recreation of canoeing and kayaking in New Zealand.

www.skabe.org Sea Kayak Association of British Columbia

www.skoanz.org.nz Sea Kayak Operators' Association of New Zealand

www2.passagen.se Sea kayaking in the Stockholm Archipelago.

www.doorway.co.za/kayak/recskasa Recreational and Commercial Sea Kayaking Association of South Africa (South Africa).

PADDLES

www.lendal.com Straight and bent-shaft touring.

www.ainsworthpaddles.com Racing and touring composite and RIM paddles.

www.aquabound.com Touring paddles.

www.atpaddle.com Adventure Technology composite touring paddles.

www.betsiebaykayak.com Greenland-style paddles.

www.bigspoons.com Lightweight touring paddles.

www.wildfur.com/paddles Sea kayaking paddles.

www.paddles.com Composite kayak touring paddles.

www.maloneofmaine.com Wood one- and two-piece touring paddles.

www.mitchellpaddles.com Sea kayaking and touring paddles made of wood.

www.nimbuspaddles.com Canadian maker of fibreglass, wood and composite touring paddles.

www.kayaker.com Perception composite and wooden touring.

www.eddyline.com Composite touring paddles in fibreglass and graphite.

www.wernerpaddles.com Composite touring paddles in fibreglass and graphite combinations.

www.glenburn.care4free.net Greenland-style sea kayaking paddles.

LINKS

www.aqua.net.au/aqua/index Australian marine directory.

http://boatbuilding.com The Internet boat building, design and repair resource for amateurs and professionals.

www.kayakist.com/BrucesPaddlingPage Contains links to both sea and whitewater kayaking, as well as good general resources.

www.gorp.com/gorp/activity/paddle A large list of links to whitewater and sea kayaking sources.

www.ilena.demon.co.uk A link list with mostly British and US sources.

www.ckf.org/Paddling Very large compilation of links presented by the California Kayak Friends.

www.kayakonline.com Extensive list of links to sea kayaks and sea kayaking gear.

www.tky.hut.fi/~teepakki/kayak/kayak_links Kayaking links from all over the world.

www.paddles.com Links to a wide variety of paddling sources, both sea kayaking and whitewater.

www.cyber-dyne.com/~jkohnen/boatlink Extremely large list of links.

www.adfdell.pstc.brown.edu/kayak Large list of links to outfitters and retailers (mostly in the USA).

http://155.187.10.12/jrc/kayak/others.html An enormous list of links from Australia.

www.wavelengthmagazine.com A geographic and alphabetic index to paddling guides, outfitters, retailers, manufacturers and clubs.

MANUFACTURERS OF SEA KAYAKING GEAR

www.acekayak.com Plastic touring kayaks manufactured in the UK.

www.kayaker.com Plastic and composite sea kayaks.

www.betsiebaykayak.com Touring kayaks made of a lightweight marine plywood/epoxy/fibreglass composite and paddles based on Greenland Inuit designs.

www.borealdesign.com Canadian maker of fibreglass, kevlar and carbon sea kayaks and paddles.

www.thomassondesign.com Swedish maker of wooden touring kayaks.

www.clcboats.com Wooden sea kayak plans and kits.

www.cdkayak.com Plastic and composite sea kayaks.

www.dagger.com Plastic and composite sea kayaks.

www.easyriderkayaks.com Composite and royalex sea kayaks.

www.eddyline.com Composite sea kayaks, paddles.

www.hem.passagen.se Swedish maker of sea kayaks.

www.greatcanadian.com Sea kayaks, including tandem boats.

www.greenval.com Kayaks and kayak building plans for strip-built and composite boats.

www.gokajaksport.com Composite sea kayaks and kayak accessories.

www.kirton-kayaks.co.uk Maker of composite racing and touring kayaks.

www.canoesandkayaks.com Composite sea kayaks in kevlar and fibreglass.

www.marinerkayaks.com Composite sea kayaks in kevlar and fibreglass.

www.marstrandskajaker.se Swedish maker of composite sea kayaks.

www.mega-kayaks.co.uk British maker of kayaks and paddles. Some sea kayaks.

www.nwkayaks.com Dennis Kayaks (NDK) Composite sea kayaks.

www.ourvision.com PandH Sea Kayaks.

www.seavivor.com Folding sea kayaks and kayak gear.

www.3aweb.com Single- and multiple-boat trailers for kayaks or canoes.

www.borealdesign.com Canadian maker of fibreglass, kevlar and carbon sea kayaks, fibreglass, RTM and graphite paddles.

www.kayaker.com Neoprene sprayskirts, socks, pogues and other accessories.

www.jlc.net/~hlevin Hand-held fishing rigs for kayaks and canoes.

www.garmin.com Global positioning systems and other marine products.

www.gearpro.com Basic sea kayaking gear and a wide variety of camping and outdoors gear.

www.icchi.com Sea kayak paddles and sails.

www.knoydart.co.uk An enormous amount of kayaking gear and accessories. A dealer of Valley Sea Kayaks as well.

www.knupac.com Portaging systems for kayaks and canoes.

www.magellangps.com Global positioning systems, chart plotters and other accessories.

www.maptech.com Marine navigation gear, including charts, software, plotters, cruising grids and more.

www.northwater.com Paddling equipment.

www.nookie.co.uk Cags and trousers, dry bags, throwlines, sprayskirts, paddling mitts and more.
www.nsipadz.com North Shore foam products, sprayskirts and other accessories for sea kayaks.
www.orgear.com Outdoor clothing, medical kits, travel accessories, foot and hand wear and more.
www.palm-equipment.co.uk Paddling clothing, dry systems, PFDs, ocean equipment, accessories and more.
www.patagonia.com Paddling and camping clothing and accessories.
www.kayaker.com Clothing, PFDs, helmets, flotation, sprayskirts, storage and more.
www.petzl.com Lighting for all situations and needs.
www.deluge.com Kayak carts, bike/boat trailers, pads, straps, roof racks, boat hangers, sails and countless other sea kayaking accessories.
www.thule.com Thule Car Rack Systems.
www.kayakstore.com Paddles, sprayskirts, gear bags and paddling clothing.

ONLINE SEA KAYAKING MAGAZINES AND E-ZINES

www.members.aol.com/gokayak/anorak Association of North Atlantic Kayakers.
www.canoekayak.about.com Paddling trips, reviews, buyers guides, techniques, tips, glossary of terms, online directory, links and more.
www.kanu.de Note: in German.
www.paddlermagazine.com Gear reviews, tips and tricks.
www.seakayaker.com Photos, stories, classified ads, tips and tricks.
www.seakayakermag.com An online link to the premier sea kayaking publication in the USA.
www.wavelengthmagazine.com

GLOSSARY

aft toward the stern.

aid to navigation a buoy, daymark or light that assists navigators.

back face the face of the paddle blade that normally faces the bow and usually has a strengthening rib extending from the paddle shaft.

barrier beach a sandbar oriented generally parallel to the shore that remains dry at high tide and protects a body of salt water behind it from ocean waves.

Beaufort wind scale a scale that describes the sea state at a given range of wind speed.

beam on the side or width of the kayak.

bongo slide occurs when the kayak is turned sideways onto a wave and is bounced towards the beach.

bow the forward part or front end of the kayak.

brace a technique allowing an off-balance kayaker to recover stability by pushing the paddle blade against the water's surface to generate force.

breaker a breaking wave.

cam cleat a releasable attachment on the rear of the kayak for towing.

capsize an event where a kayak, with the kayaker inside, overturns in the water.

chart a nautical chart; a map of the sea.

chart datum the reference, or '0' water level on a nautical chart. Usually set at the level of the lowest astronomical tide.

circumnavigate to travel, by water, entirely around a piece of land, such as an island.

clapotis explosive waves formed when waves from two different directions collide.

coaming the moulded ridge surrounding the cockpit, allowing attachment of the spray deck/skirt.

cockpit open area in the centre of the kayak where the kayaker sits.

compass rose two concentric circles on a chart, each subdivided into 360 degrees, showing the directions of true north and magnetic north.

dead reckoning navigational technique in which course, speed and time underway are used to deduce an estimated position.

deck the upper surface of the kayak.

deck lines rope or bungees strung along the deck to allow storage of gear.

distress signal an internationally recognized signal used by a vessel to request help.

diurnal tide a tide cycle with one high and one low tide per day.

draw stroke a stroke using the power face to propel the boat sideways.

drybag a waterproof storage container designed for gear that you wish to keep dry.

drysuit a completely watertight, full-body garment that decreases heat loss when the wearer is submerged in water.

ebb outgoing tide.

feathering angle at which blades are set in relation to one another.

fetch unimpeded distance over which the wind can blow; a longer fetch allows the formation of larger waves.

flood incoming tide.

following wind/sea a wind/sea blowing in the direction of travel.

gradient the steepness of the shoreline.

hatch a closable storage area within a kayak.

headtorch a light source strapped to the forehead, freeing the hands for use.

headland a steep-sided point of land that projects out from a coast into deep water.

headwind a wind blowing opposite the direction of travel.

high tide   the event occurring when the water level is at its highest point during a tide cycle.

hull   the lower surface of the kayak that sits in the water.

intertidal zone   that land covered by water at high tide but exposed at low tide, shown in green on the chart.

isobars   lines on a weather map joining places of equal pressure.

knot   a unit of speed equivalent to one nautical mile per hour.

lee shore   when you are on the water, the shore toward which the wind is blowing; the lee of an island, on the other hand, is the downwind side protected from the wind.

low tide   the event occurring when the water level is at its lowest point during a tide cycle.

lunar day   the time between consecutive meridian passages of the moon, equivalent to 24 hours 50 minutes.

magnetic north   the direction toward which a compass points. The difference in angle between true north and magnetic north is called variation. Navigational compass directions are assumed to reference magnetic north unless noted otherwise.

marine weather forecast   a weather forecast predicting conditions on a body of water, emphasizing those factors that affect navigation or safety of mariners.

nautical mile   1 nautical mile, equal to 1 minute of latitude; approximately 1.9km.

open sea/water   any salt water not protected from waves or swells originating at sea; waters receiving the full force of ocean weather.

paddling speed   the speed of your kayak relative to the water in which you are paddling, usually averaged over a period of time.

painter   a rope mounted on a kayak used to secure the kayak on shore.

personal flotation device (PFD)   a buoyant article of clothing worn to keep the wearer afloat when in the water.

port   the left hand side.

power/drive face   the face of the paddle blade that normally faces the stern and usually has a concave shape.

protected water   those parts of the ocean that experience diminished waves or swells, usually due to intervening land. The water defined as 'protected' changes depending on the wind direction.

range/transit   a line drawn through two points of fixed position used to identify position.

reverse stroke   a stroke using the back face to propel the kayak backward.

rip current   a current flowing away from a beach that is caused by excess water input from waves breaking on the beach returning out to sea.

rocker   when looking at a kayak from the beam, the curvature of the bottom of the hull.

salt marsh   a tidal body of water lying behind a barrier beach, protected from ocean waves and containing extensive grassland in the intertidal zone.

semidiurnal tide   a tide cycle with two high and two low tides per day.

shipping lane   an area designated for the travel of large, ocean-going vessels.

shoal   a shallow area in a waterway caused by the deposition of sediment.

slack water   the event occurring when the speed of a tidal current reaches a minimum. Also known simply as slack.

sounding   a chart mark indicating the depth of water.

soup   area of white water in the surf zone, inshore of the main break.

speed over ground   the speed of your kayak relative to a fixed point like the ocean bottom or shoreline.

spray deck/skirt   a waterproof article of clothing worn around the kayaker's waist and attached to the cockpit coaming to prevent the entry of water into the cockpit.

spring tide   a tide with a relatively large tide range, occurring twice each month when the sun and the moon align.

squall   sudden gust of wind.

starboard   the right-hand side.

statute mile   a measurement of distance equivalent to 5,280ft, or 0.87 nautical miles. Usually used on land and while navigating fresh water.

stern   the rear part or back end of the kayak.

surf   (1) waves breaking on shore or on an underwater object; (2) to ride a wave.

sweep stroke a stroke using the power face (forward sweep) or the back face (reverse sweep) to turn the kayak.

swell organized waves that were generated in faraway storms.

tidal influenced by the tides.

tidal stream/current the movement of water caused by the tides.

tidal stream/current predictions a table showing predicted times and velocities of both slack water and maximum flood and ebb currents for a given location.

tide the regular increase and decrease of water levels on the ocean.

tide tables/predictions a table of forecasted times and heights of high and low tides for a given location.

topographic map a map of a region of land showing elevation, contours, buildings, bodies of water, and roads. Not designed for navigation on water. Official topographic maps in the US are produced by the US Geological Survey.

tow line a rope mounted on a kayak/kayaker to enable the towing of another kayak.

true north the direction pointing toward the geographic north pole of the earth. Longitude lines point directly toward true north. Directions given relative to true north should be noted, for example, '195 degrees true'.

weather to a mariner, weather consists of wind, ocean swells, rain, and fog.

INDEX